Teaching the Diary of
Anne Frank

An In-Depth Resource for Learning About the Holocaust Through the Writings of Anne Frank

by Susan Moger

SCHOLASTIC
PROFESSIONAL BOOKS

New York ■ Toronto ■ London ■ Auckland ■ Sydney ■ Mexico City ■ New Delhi ■ Hong Kong

Acknowledgments

I am indebted to many people for their help in the creation of this book: to Terry Cooper and Liza Charlesworth of Scholastic Professional Books for entrusting me with this assignment; to Iris Sroka, Ph.D, for her vision of what this book could be and her thoughtful comments as it developed; to Elaine Israel for a masterful editing job; and to our advisory board—Dr. Adele Brodkin, Paula Jasser, Meryl Menashe, Sid Reischer, and Laura Robb—for their valuable suggestions. I am also grateful to the designers, Ellen Hassell and Manuel Rivera of Boultinghouse & Boultinghouse, and to photo researcher, Deborah Kurosz, for bringing the book to life.

I would also like to acknowledge Harry and Fanny Reischer, who fought as partisans during the Holocaust and whose children and grandchildren are an ongoing celebration of life. *L'Chaim!*

Scholastic Inc. grants teachers permission to photocopy the reproducible pages from this book for classroom use. No other part of this publication may be reproduced in whole or in part, or stored in a retrieval system, or transmitted in any form or by any means, electronic, mechanical, photocopying, recording, or otherwise, without written permission of the publisher. For information regarding permission, write to Scholastic Inc., 555 Broadway, New York, NY 10012.

Edited by Elaine Israel

Design by Ellen Matlach Hassell for Boultinghouse & Boultinghouse, Inc.

Illustration Credits Cover: Mona Mark; Interior: pp. 38–39, 55, 71: Manuel Rivera

Photo research by Deborah Kurosz

Photo Credits pp. 1, 6, 7, 12, 30 (top), 31, 32, 33 (bottom), 34 (bottom), 35 (bottom), 36, 37 (bottom), 42, 43, 44, 49, 54, 55, 72, 89, 94: © AFF/Anne Frank Stichting, Amsterdam; pp. 35 (top), 37 (top both), 47, 59, 77: Rijksinstituut voor Oorloggsdocumentatie, Amsterdam; pp. 21, 75, 97: Corbis-Bettmann; pp. 29, 33 (top right), 82: Hulton Getty/Liaison Agency; p. 30 (bottom): Courtesy Elaine Israel; p. 34 (top): © 1998 JP Owen/Black Star; pp. 26, 33 (top left), 50, 58, 68, 80: UPI/Corbis-Bettmann; p. 53: © Baitel/Landmann—Gamma Liaison; p. 86: Courtesy of USHMM Photo Archives; p. 87: Wide World Photos; p. 92: © Thirteen/WNET; p. 98: © Rick Friedman/Black Star

ISBN: 0-590-67482-X

Contents

Preface

I was born on the day Anne Frank went into hiding—July 6, 1942. When I first read *The Diary of a Young Girl*, I was 13, the same age as Anne when she started her diary. That combination of events, and the fact that I, too, kept a diary, forged a connection between Anne and me. But it was a connection I kept to myself. I don't recall discussing Anne's book with anyone. When I saw the play *The Diary of Anne Frank* in 1956, I was numbed by the hammering on the door that signals the end—the end of the play, the end of the diary, the end of Anne's life—but I had no idea how or where—or why—Anne died.

There was a wall of silence around what happened after the diary ended. Today that wall of silence has been pierced. Most editions of the diary provide readers with detailed information about Anne's last days and the fates of the others in the Secret Annexe. Even the police officer who arrested them has been identified and brought to trial. But despite this wealth of information, readers today are still haunted by the question *Why*? Why were Anne and her family, along with millions of others, stigmatized, deprived of their possessions, forced into hiding, hunted down, and killed?

To explore that *why* is to confront the enormity of the Holocaust. That confrontation is a moral imperative because only by facing the Holocaust can we see Anne's diary for what it is—an act of spiritual resistance to Nazi terror.

To help you and your students make connections between Anne Frank and the cataclysmic period in which she lived, I have gathered essential source materials from the period. These documents will introduce students to voices that complement Anne's. From an emotional as well as an intellectual point of view, some of the documents will be hard to read. They speak of unimaginable horror—sometimes in the chillingly matter-of-fact voice of bureaucracy, sometimes in the anguished cry of a parent who has lost a child, and sometimes in the stirring tone of resistance.

Taken together, and read along with Anne's diary, the source materials challenge us to learn more and to remember. In doing so, you will make the leap from Anne's time to today, leading students to an understanding of how hatred can never end unless we are all vigilant. Only by remembering can we ensure that in our time the evil that engulfed her and millions of others—and that stifled her brave voice—can never again take root.

Susan Moger

A Note to Teachers

The Diary of a Young Girl by Anne Frank puts a human face on faceless events; it gives a voice to silent images of destruction; it imposes life on a process consumed with death. Anne, the writer, is many things. She is an astute observer of the people around her, a storyteller who weaves insights and dreams into her accounts of daily events, and a serious historian determined to make her diary a valuable record for people after the war. Thanks to her extraordinary ability as a writer, she accomplished her goal, though she did not survive to see it.

Anne Frank

The diary not only documents Anne's two years in hiding but also sheds light on the world outside the cramped rooms of the Secret Annexe. Anne notes that despite wartime restrictions, the Franks were able to keep a radio and listened to broadcasts from London on the BBC several times a day. Because of this, they were well informed about the course of the war. For example, after the eagerly awaited Allied landings in Europe in June 1944, Anne records her hopes that Holland will be liberated soon. In her diary, Anne also reflects on news brought by Miep Gies and other visitors about events in Amsterdam and beyond, such as mass deportations of Jews, anti-Jewish feeling, and strikes against the Nazi occupiers.

Although many of the events we collectively call the Holocaust occurred outside of the Franks' experience, their fates were part of a complex mechanism of destruction set in motion long before they went into hiding and predetermined by carefully coordinated decisions. The full horror of that destructive process was not known to the Franks until after they were arrested on August 4, 1944. We have no record of Anne's reactions in her own words, only in the words of eyewitnesses. An understanding of the stages of this destructive process, which are discussed in Section 2 of this book, links the events Anne does report on in the diary—restrictions on transportation, curfews, wearing the yellow star, the deportations she hears about, her own life in hiding—with the terrible events affecting Jews all over Europe.

In this book you will find Resource Pages that present primary-source materials to help provide a picture of the Holocaust as it unfolded outside the Secret Annexe—in the offices of bureaucrats, in the ghettos, and inside the killing centers. The words in these documents are important for students to read and understand—whether they are the bland doublespeak of official documents, the cry of a father for his doomed child, or the dispassionate description of a gas chamber at Auschwitz-Birkenau by two men who escaped. The words in these Resource Pages call to us from more than 50 years ago. They create a context for the diary, a vantage point from which readers can appreciate the true nature of the horror that inched ever closer to the Franks between 1940 and 1945.

Using This Book

This book will guide you in enriching students' reading of the diary and in placing it in the context of the Holocaust. As students read through Anne's diary, this book will help you enhance the experience with discussion questions, journal prompts, Resource Pages, and projects, including keeping a response journal. Because you best know students' learning styles, the suggestions are meant to be flexible guidelines.

Anne Frank's diary

Teaching About the Holocaust

Learning about the Holocaust can be a profoundly disturbing experience. Teaching about it can be upsetting, too. You are dealing with a subject that is unlike any you have ever encountered. Current newspapers often have articles about people's inhumanity toward one another. But the Holocaust offers another dimension to human depravity and may alter students' views of the world.

Students respond to this information in different ways—by being upset, by refusing to accept it, by adopting a stance of unconcern. Sparing students' feelings by watering down the information is a disservice to them, to those who suffered and died in the Holocaust, and to those who survived.

Using *The Diary of a Young Girl* to teach about the Holocaust can seem at first to intensify the difficulty. Students become acquainted with Anne Frank through her engaging writer's voice and her strong, distinctive personality only to learn that her individualism, her writing, and finally her life were extinguished by the horror the Nazi regime unleashed on the world.

What is a child or adult confronted with this history for the first time to make of it? How can we ask young people to perform the brutal calculations of multiplying Anne's fate six million times? How do we and students make sense of the Holocaust? And, though we must move on to other subjects after studying about it, can we do so without being forever changed?

Here are some suggestions as you begin your study.

- Let students know that you are going to be learning *with* them as you embark on your study of the Holocaust. At times, this may mean crying and expressing anguish together. Tears and grief are natural as you share your feelings. The journals, which students will submit for your review, can help you be more aware of students' understanding and concerns about the material. As you share your own journal entries with students, you will also empathize with them.

- Deal immediately with students who respond to learning about the Holocaust by becoming attracted to the symbols of Nazi power— swastika, salutes, uniforms, special greetings. Show how these symbols were used to manipulate millions of people into acceptance of the horrors of the Holocaust.

- Invite survivors of the Holocaust to speak to your class. A person who "steps out of history" into the present helps to put a human face on the Holocaust. Expressing their feelings and asking questions of survivors is a way for young people to connect with events that took place long ago.

- "Spiritual resistance" is an important theme in your study of the Holocaust. While armed resistance and sabotage were means of attacking the Nazis, those who recorded events, celebrated Jewish holidays, and maintained loving relationships in the face of evil were also resisters. Readers of the diary honor Anne Frank's life and acknowledge her dedication to spiritual resistance. The very act of learning about the Holocaust helps you and students disprove the Nazis' contention that the world would not care about the fate of the Jews or believe in the realities of the "final solution."

- Individual responsibility is another important theme. Individuals carried out the Holocaust, either by taking an active role or by silently acquiescing in the killing of millions of people. Individuals also resisted the Holocaust. By learning about them, we strengthen the part of ourselves that can identify and resist evil.

- By learning about the Holocaust, we may prevent it ever happening again. Students can overcome feelings of powerlessness by vowing to be vigilant in identifying scapegoating, bigotry, and state-sanctioned violence against groups of people.

Keep parents informed and involved as you proceed with your study of the Holocaust. Copy the letter on page 12 and send it home with students. Invite parents to class when a Holocaust survivor comes to speak.

How This Book Is Organized

Section 1 introduces students to the Holocaust through Eve Bunting's allegory, *Terrible Things*. The complete text of the book introduces the concept of individual responsibility in face of attacks on others. "First They Came for the Jews," a poem by Martin Niemoller, and Recognizing Stereotyping, Scapegoating, Prejudice, and Discrimination will help students bridge the gap between the allegory and the actual events of the Holocaust.

Section 2, Defining the Holocaust, gives definitions and a glossary along with information essential for understanding the diary.

In **Section 3**, Introducing Anne Frank, the illustrated time line chronicles key events in the Frank family's life and events in the Holocaust and World War II.

Section 4, Understanding the Diary, divides the diary entries into six parts, or readings. Source materials on the Holocaust are provided as reproducible pages with each reading. These materials include firsthand accounts of victims of the Holocaust as well as official evidence of how their fate was manipulated. You will also read about cases of spiritual resistance. The juxtaposition of these examples helps students appreciate the complexity of the topic and the value of Anne's diary (itself an example of spiritual resistance).

Each of the six Readings in Section 4 includes guided reading and discussion questions and suggestions for Response Journal entries. The Response Journal, introduced in Section 4, is an important tool for studying Anne Frank's diary.

Section 5, The End of a Life, describes what took place after Anne Frank, her family, and friends were arrested on August 4, 1944. This section also includes a short history of the diary.

Section 6, Extension Projects and Resources, suggest positive steps students can take to understand and promote tolerance of different points of view and acceptance of others. These activities bring Anne's strong, positive message into the present to counteract feelings of powerlessness and despair. This section also provides an annotated list of print, video, online, and organizational resources, as well as a Glossary.

What Should Students Learn About?

You know best what's right for your students, so it's a good idea for you to read through the Resource Pages in this book to see which material is appropriate (based on students' grade and developmental level). The Planning Matrix on page 11 will help guide your selection.

This book is flexible. You can work through all of the activities in sequence (which is recommended), or make use of selected components, such as individual Resource Pages. Read and discuss them in groups or as a whole class. Distribute the pages for one-time use, then collect and reuse them. Or store them in students' folders or portfolios. Encourage students to discuss what they are reading and learning with their parents or other adults.

Boxes with background information about specific people and events are scattered throughout this book. You can read them aloud with students to provide even more depth. We suggest that you also read portions of the diary out loud with your class and discuss the diary entries before you distribute and discuss the source materials.

Planning Matrix

Section	Best for Grade(s)	Class Periods
1 Building a Context to Study the Holocaust	5 up	2
Resource Pages: Terrible Things: An Allegory of the Holocaust	5 up	
First They Came for the Jews	5 up	
Recognizing Stereotypes	5 up	
2 Defining the Holocaust	5 up	2–3
Resource Page: How the Holocaust Progressed	5 up	
3 Introducing Anne Frank	5 up	2–3
Resource Pages: A Frank Family Album	5 up	
Time Line: Anne Frank's World—1914–1945	5 up	
Maps: The Expansion of Germany	5 up	
4 Understanding the Diary		
READING 1: Diary Entries June 14, 1942–July 11, 1942	5 up	4
Resource Pages: Evaluating Sources	5 up	
Discrimination Against Jewish People	6 up	
Laws Against Jewish People	6 up	
READING 2: Diary Entries August 14, 1942–November 9, 1942	5 up	4
Resource Pages: Moment of Decision	5 up	
The Secret Annexe	5 up	
About Language at War	5 up	
Language at War	5 up	
A "Complete Solution"	6 up	
READING 3: Diary Entries November 10, 1942–June 13, 1943	5 up	3
Resource Pages: Excerpt from the Wannsee Protocol, 1/20/42	6 up	
The Nameless Numbers Speak	5 up	
Hitler Orders Silence	6 up	
READING 4: Diary Entries June 15, 1943–December 29, 1943	6 up	3
Resource Pages: Call for Diaries in the Warsaw Ghetto	5 up	
I Want My Little Daughter to Be Remembered	5 up	
The Butterfly	6 up	
READING 5: Diary Entries January 2, 1944–March 28, 1944	5 up	3
Resource Pages: Homeless	6 up	
A Dead Child Speaks	6 up	
Eyewitnesses at Auschwitz-Birkenau	6 up	
Jenny Misuchin—Jewish Resistance Fighter	5 up	
READING 6: Diary Entries March 29, 1944–August 1, 1944	5 up	2
Resource Pages: All They Had Left	5 up	
Inventory	6 up	
A Cartload of Shoes	6 up	
5 The End of a Life		4–5
Resource Pages: Discovery and Arrest	5 up	
The Last Months	6 up	
Final Meeting	6 up	
Anne's Legacy	5 up	
The Diary in the World	5 up	
6 Extension Projects and Resources	5 up	Vary

Dear Families,

Our class is starting a unit on Anne Frank's *The Diary of a Young Girl* and the Holocaust. Anne Frank's diary, first published in English in 1952, is one of the world's most treasured books. It has been translated into more than 55 languages and has sold more than 20 million copies. Putting the diary in the context of the Holocaust helps students translate faceless statistics into the experience of a specific person, a teenager like themselves, with dreams and plans, anxieties and sorrows, and a love for life. In learning about Anne's life and death, we will be considering events that took place more than 50 years ago but that have immediate relevance today.

Learning about the Holocaust helps students

- understand the danger of remaining uninvolved in the face of attacks on others' rights.

- gain a perspective on the ways a modern industrial nation used technology and governmental bureaucracy to crush dissent and carry out mass murder based on bigotry and hate.

- take responsibility, as a citizens of a democracy, for maintaining an open, tolerant society and safeguarding democratic institutions and values.

In studying the Holocaust, students face up to issues of fairness, justice, peer pressure, and conformity—issues they confront in their daily lives.

Please talk with your son or daughter about the Holocaust. Ask your child what he or she is learning. Listen to your child's reactions to the material being read. Join in learning more about the period. I welcome your comments and questions.

Sincerely,

Teaching the Diary of Anne Frank Scholastic Professional Books

Building a Context to Study the Holocaust

Terrible Things: An Allegory of the Holocaust

Give each student or small groups of students copies of pages 15–18. Having the book in class will make this activity even more effective.

❖ Getting Started

Terrible Things is an award-winning picture book illustrated with black-and-white drawings. The Terrible Things of the title are never distinctly shown. They always appear as swirling dark clouds that sometimes suggest human shapes and at other times suggest huge, menacing animals.

An allegory is a picture or story that has a meaning beyond the one conveyed in the obvious story line. *Terrible Things* is a good starting point for trying to help students understand what happened during the Holocaust.

Together, read the Terrible Things Resource Pages. Suggest that students take turns reading the roles of Little Rabbit, Big Rabbit, and the other animals.

After your class has had a chance to reflect on what they've just read, spend time on the discussion questions.

Then ask students to list on the chalkboard some of the questions Little Rabbit asks about the Terrible Things and the answers Big Rabbit gives.

Little Rabbit's Questions

- "Why did the Terrible Things want the birds?"
- "What's wrong with feathers?"
- "But why did the Terrible Things take them away?"
- "Do the Terrible Things want the clearing for themselves?"

Big Rabbit's Responses

- "We mustn't ask."
- "The Terrible Things don't need a reason."
- "Be glad it wasn't us."
- "Just mind your own business."
- "We don't want them to get mad at us."

Ask students:
What is Big Rabbit trying to tell Little Rabbit? Do the answers satisfy Little Rabbit? How can you tell? What answers would you give to Little Rabbit's questions? What other questions would you ask?

What does the story imply about non-Jews' reactions to the fate of the Jews and others during the Holocaust?

❖ Projects

Have students work individually or in groups to:

- retell the story as a poem.

- adapt the story as a play or Reader's Theater.

- write the next chapter and answer these questions: Where does Little Rabbit go? How does he "tell other forest creatures"? What happens then?

❖ Resource Pages

Terrible Things: An Allegory of the Holocaust (pages 15–18)

First They Came for the Jews (page 19)

Recognizing Stereotyping, Scapegoating, Prejudice, and Discrimination (pages 20–22)

Terrible Things

An Allegory of
the Holocaust

by Eve Bunting

In Europe, during World War II, many people looked the other way while terrible things happened. They pretended not to know that their neighbors were being taken away and imprisoned in concentration camps. They pretended not to hear cries for help. The Nazis killed millions of Jews and others in the Holocaust. If everyone had stood together at the first sign of evil would this have happened?

Standing up for what you know is right is not always easy. Especially if the one you face is bigger and stronger than you. It is easier to look the other way. But, if you do, terrible things can happen.

—E. B.

The clearing in the woods was home to the small forest creatures. The birds and squirrels shared the trees. The rabbits and porcupines shared the shade beneath the trees and the frogs and fish shared the cool brown waters of the forest pond.

Until the day the Terrible Things came. Little Rabbit saw their terrible shadows before he saw them. They stopped at the edge of the clearing and their shadows blotted out the sun.

"We have come for every creature with feathers on its back," the Terrible Things thundered.

"We don't have feathers," the frogs said.

"Nor we," said the squirrels.

"Nor we," said the porcupines.

"Nor we," said the rabbits.

The little fish leaped from the water to show the shine of their scales, but the birds twittered nervously in the tops of the trees. Feathers! They rose in the air, then screamed away into the blue of the sky.

But the Terrible Things had brought their terrible nets, and they flung them high and caught the birds and carried them away.

The other forest creatures talked nervously among themselves.
"Those birds were always noisy," Old Porcupine said. "Good riddance, I say."

"There's more room in the trees now," the squirrels said.

"Why did the Terrible Things want the birds?" asked Little Rabbit. "What's wrong with feathers?"

"We mustn't ask," Big Rabbit said. "The Terrible Things don't need a reason. Just be glad it wasn't us they wanted."

Now there were no birds to sing in the clearing. But life went on almost as before. Until the day the Terrible Things came back.

"We have come for every creature with bushy tails," roared the Terrible Things.

"We have no tails," the frogs said.

"Nor do we. Not real tails," the porcupines said.

The little fish jumped from the water to show the smooth shine of their finned tails and the rabbits turned their rumps so the Terrible Things could see for themselves.

"Our tails are round and furry," they said. "By no means are they bushy."

The squirrels chattered their fear and ran high into the treetops. But the Terrible Things swung their terrible nets higher than the squirrels could run and wider than the squirrels could leap and they caught them all and carried them away.

"Those squirrels were greedy," Big Rabbit said. "Always storing away things for themselves. Never sharing."

"But why did the Terrible Things take them away?" Little Rabbit asked. "Do the Terrible Things want the clearing for themselves?"

"No. They have their own place," Big Rabbit said. "But the Terrible Things don't need a reason. Just mind your own business, Little Rabbit. We don't want them to get mad at us."

Now there were no birds to sing or squirrels to chatter in the trees. But life in the clearing went on almost as before. Until the day the Terrible Things came again.

Little Rabbit heard the rumble of their terrible voices.

"We have come for every creature that swims," the Terrible Things thundered.

"Oh, we can't swim," the rabbits said quickly.

"And we can't swim," the porcupines said.

The frogs dived deep in the forest pool and ripples spiraled like

Teaching the Diary of Anne Frank   Scholastic Professional Books

corkscrews on the dark brown water. The little fish darted this way and that in streaks of silver. But the Terrible Things threw their terrible nets down into the depths and they dragged up the dripping frogs and the shimmering fish and carried them away.

"Why did the Terrible Things take them?" Little Rabbit asked. "What did the frogs and fish do to them?"

"Probably nothing," Big Rabbit said. "But the Terrible Things don't need a reason. Many creatures dislike frogs. Lumpy slimy things. And fish are so cold and unfriendly. They never talk to any of us."

Now there were no birds to sing, no squirrels to chatter, no frogs to croak, no fish to play in the forest pool. A nervous silence filled the clearing. But life went on almost as usual. Until the day the Terrible Things came back.

Little Rabbit smelled their terrible smell before they came into sight. The rabbits and the porcupines looked all around, everywhere, except at each other.

"We have come for every creature that sprouts quills," the Terrible Things thundered.

The rabbits stopped quivering. "We don't have quills," they said, fluffing their soft, white fur.

The porcupines bristled with all their strength. But the Terrible Things covered them with the their terrible nets, and the porcupines hung in them like flies in a spider's web as the Terrible Things carried them away.

"Those porcupines always were bad tempered," Big Rabbit said shakily. "Prickly, sticky things!"

This time Little Rabbit didn't ask why. By now he knew that the Terrible Things didn't need a reason. The Terrible Things had gone, but the smell still filled the clearing.

"I liked it better when there were all kinds of creatures in our clearing," he said. "And I think we should move. What if the Terrible Things come back?"

"Nonsense," said Big Rabbit. "Why should we move? This has always been our home. And the Terrible Things won't come back. We are White Rabbits. It couldn't happen to us."

As day followed day Little Rabbit thought Big Rabbit must be right. Until the day the Terrible Things came back.

Little Rabbit saw the terrible gleam of their terrible eyes through the forest darkness. And he smelled the terrible smell.

"We have come for any creature that is white," the Terrible Things thundered.

"There are no white creatures here but us," Big Rabbit said.

"We have come for you," the Terrible Things said.

The rabbits scampered in every direction. "Help!" they cried. "Somebody help!" But there was no one left to help. And the big, circling nets dropped over them, and the Terrible Things carried them away.

All but Little Rabbit, who was little enough to hide in a pile of rocks by the pond and smart enough to stay so still that the Terrible Things thought he was a rock himself.

When they had all gone, Little Rabbit crept into the middle of the empty clearing. "I should have tried to help the other rabbits," he thought. "If only we creatures had stuck together, it could have been different."

Sadly, Little Rabbit left the clearing. He'd go tell other forest creatures about the Terrible Things. He hoped someone would listen.

Talk It Over

1. Why do you think the author told the story of the Holocaust in this symbolic way? Who is this story directed to?

2. Why do you think the Terrible Things take away the animals one group at a time?

3. In an allegory, people, places, and events are used as symbols. What can the clearing in the woods stand for? What about the different animals? The Terrible Things?

4. What kind of excuses do the other animals offer to explain the fate of each group as it is taken away? How do these reactions help the Terrible Things?

5. How are the Terrible Things described? What verbs are used to describe their actions? How do the descriptions affect your feelings about the Terrible Things?

6. During the Holocaust, terrible things were done by real people, people with faces, names, and life histories. Why do you think the author shows the Terrible Things as anonymous?

7. What choices do the animals in the clearing have when the Terrible Things come?

8. What would you say to Big Rabbit's statement, "We are the White Rabbits. It couldn't happen to us"?

9. When the Terrible Things come for the rabbits, what do the rabbits do? What choice does Little Rabbit make? Why? What does this tell you about the Terrible Things?

10. Little Rabbit hopes someone will listen to him. Why might no one listen?

Teaching the Diary of Anne Frank   Scholastic Professional Books

First They Came for the Jews

Martin Niemoller was a German pastor and theologian born in Lippstadt, Germany, in 1892. Niemoller was an anti-Communist and, for that reason, supported Hitler's rise to power—at first. But when Hitler insisted on the supremacy of the state over religion, Niemoller became disillusioned. He became the leader of a group of German clergymen opposed to Hitler. Unlike Niemoller, they gave in to the Nazis' threats. Hitler personally detested Niemoller and had him arrested and eventually confined in the concentration camps of Sachsenhausen and Dachau. Niemoller was released in 1945 by the Allies. He continued his career in Germany as a clergyman and noted pacifist.

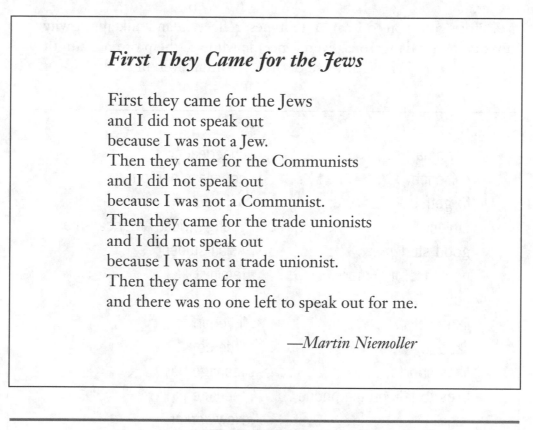

First They Came for the Jews

First they came for the Jews
and I did not speak out
because I was not a Jew.
Then they came for the Communists
and I did not speak out
because I was not a Communist.
Then they came for the trade unionists
and I did not speak out
because I was not a trade unionist.
Then they came for me
and there was no one left to speak out for me.

—*Martin Niemoller*

Talk It Over

1. At the end of the poem, why is there "no one left" to speak for the narrator?

2. Sometimes poems make us happy. Sometimes they make us sad. How does this poem make you feel?

3. How is this poem like *Terrible Things*? How is it different?

"First They Came for the Jews" by Pastor Martin Niemoller appears in *Holocaust Poetry* edited by Hilda Schiff, St. Martin's Press, 1995. Every effort has been made to trace the copyright owners of this work.

Recognizing Stereotyping, Scapegoating, Prejudice, and Discrimination

A half-hour situation comedy usually doesn't have time to give characters much depth. So the writers often draw them in broad strokes instead of making them stand out as individuals. Below are adjectives that are sometimes used to describe groups of people. The use of stereotypes persists even though we know they are mean or silly—and just plain wrong.

Before going on to Real Stereotypes, reflect on and talk about why stereotypes are dangerous, even if people who use them often claim they mean no harm. Why is any use of them harmful, even in a joke?

not smart	cheerleader
nuisance	homeless person
forgetful	old person
athletic	young African-American man
good student	Asian student
no sense of humor	feminist
cute	baby
likes dolls	little girl
likes toy cars	little boy
likes sports	teenage boy
likes to talk on the phone	teenage girl
rude	New Yorker
laid back	Californian
honest	Midwesterner
friendly, hospitable	Southerner

Teaching the Diary of Anne Frank Scholastic Professional Books

Real Stereotypes

Real stereotypes are not funny. They are harmful and hurtful. They keep us from seeing people as individuals. Stereotypes are especially dangerous when they determine how people act toward one another.

In the 1930s in Germany, the Nazis used **stereotypes** of Jews to turn other Germans against them. Posters with hateful stereotypes of Jewish people—showing exaggerated features such as big noses and greedy expressions—were common. Frustrated by losing World War I and by the economic problems they then faced during the Great Depression, many Germans needed someone to blame. The Nazis picked up on this. To take the public's attention off them, even before they came to power in 1933, the Nazis blamed Germany's problems on "international Jewry." Jews everywhere, not just in Germany, were blamed for the economic conditions, even for losing the war.

Germany had a totalitarian government in which all sources of information were controlled. But even if that hadn't been true, Germans needed someone to blame. They were easily persuaded to make Jewish people scapegoats for their problems.

Scapegoating, or attributing blame, works because it gives people a focus for their frustrations and their anger and gives them a reason for their prejudices.

Scapegoating doesn't have to be based on fact for it to work. Neither does prejudice. Many Germans and people in other countries were prejudiced against Jews for all kinds of reasons that didn't make sense. **Prejudice** is strong feelings that can be difficult to change. People who hate a certain group often have never actually met a member of that group.

Discrimination is prejudice in action. Discrimination is a way to exclude or abuse people for reasons that make no sense—usually because of their race, religion, nationality, or anything else that sets them apart. Discrimination requires action on the part of the person who discriminates. That's why it is easier to identify someone who discriminates than someone who is prejudiced.

A prewar poster on a German street portrayed a nasty stereotype of Jewish people.

Read this dialogue. Why doesn't Mo make sense? Have you ever met anyone like Mo? What would you say to Mo if you were the third person taking part in this dialogue?

Stereotype

MO: Purple people are always thieves.

JO: Why do you say that?

Scapegoating

MO: Well, someone told me he heard that a purple person was nearby when Mr. Smith lost his wallet. It's a purple person's fault that Mr. Smith has no money.

JO: Maybe he dropped it or left it somewhere.

Prejudice

MO: Come on. It had to have been one of the purple people. That's how purple people are.

JO: I don't see how you can say that.

Discrimination

MO: I've heard that purple people always seem to have money. So one of them probably stole the wallet.

JO: Have you actually ever met or spoken to a purple person?

MO: No. But I hate them anyway! That's why I won't be friends with them.

Talk It Over

1. Think of the TV shows you watch. How many stereotypes can you identify on them? Are they meant to show prejudice? Are they meant in a mean-spirited way? If not, why are they still damaging?

2. Is it easier to create TV characters that fit a mold than to come up with distinctive characters? Why or why not?

3. Why do the words *stereotyping*, *scapegoating*, *prejudice*, and *discrimination* usually go together?

4. What would you do if you met a person like Mo? Is there anything more that Jo could have done to help the situation?

5. Can you identify the stereotypes used in *Terrible Things* to justify the disappearance of various animals?

Teaching the Diary of Anne Frank   Scholastic Professional Books

A Brief History of Anti-Semitism

The term *anti-Semitism* was first used in the nineteenth century by Walter Marr, a German. He used it to mean "hatred of Jews and Judaism." But Marr misused it. The word *Semitic* actually refers to a group of languages, not to a group of people. Semitic languages include Arabic, Aramaic, Amharic, and Hebrew. Marr's form continues to be wrongly used to mean anti-Jewish feeling and actions.

Even before Christianity, there was anti-Semitism. The Jewish people's unbending belief in one God offended the Greeks and Romans, who worshiped many gods. The early Christian church treated Jews harshly, blaming them for the death of Christ (who was himself a Jew).

During the Middle Ages, the armies of the First Crusade marched across Europe to liberate the Holy Land from Muslims. As part of their holy mission to stamp out "unbelievers," the Crusaders murdered European Jews.

For about 300 years, from the eleventh to the fourteenth century, Jews were tolerated as businesspeople in most Christian communities. This was often because their businesses were essential. But as outsiders, they were always subject to rumors and hate campaigns. In the fifteenth century, Jewish people who refused to convert were among the victims of the Inquisition, a bloody campaign to make Spain a Catholic nation. The hatred continued after the Protestant Reformation, although some Protestant sects were more tolerant of Jews than the Catholic Church was. In parts of Europe, Jews were forced to live in ghettos, separate from Christians. During the Enlightenment of the eighteenth century, Jews gained more political freedom, often at the price of their religious observances.

In nineteenth-century Europe, a more tolerant atmosphere led to the acceptance of Jewish people, again at the price of their religious practices. Jews who became assimilated in an attempt to fit in with their Christian neighbors often gave up their traditional religious practices. In the late nineteenth century, some Jewish people reacted against this trend. To assure the continuation of Judaism and to protect themselves, some Jews began the Zionist movement. Zionists dreamed of establishing a Jewish state in Palestine.

Anti-Semitism again became more prevalent in the late nineteenth and early twentieth centuries. Using trumped-up scientific evidence that made a mockery of science, people who called themselves experts said the Jewish people were an inferior race. Nationalists in many countries embraced these racial theories and regarded Jews as lesser citizens compared to "pure" French, German, or Russian citizens.

In Russia, Jews fell victim to massacres called pogroms. It was not unusual for Jewish families to flee under cover of night. That was one reason they tended to be in businesses that could be easily moved.

Anti-Semitism based on economic worries fueled suspicions of wealthy Jewish families like the Rothschilds, who were bankers. Jews were blamed for all kinds of problems, especially those having to do with money.

In reaction to this virulent anti-Semitism based on race, many Jews and non-Jews insisted that Judaism was a religion. They said it was like any other and that Jews were as French, Russian, or German as other citizens. After World War I, some Germans blamed the Jews for Germany's defeat, ignoring the fact that many Jews had fought bravely for their country.

Anti-Semitism became less important in Germany during the mid- to late 1920s when good economic times returned. But with the start of the Great Depression in 1929, hard times fueled the flames of the violent anti-Semitism spread by Adolf Hitler and his National Socialist (Nazi) Party. With Hitler's political victory in 1933, anti-Semitism became government policy. Eventually, at the cost of millions of lives, the murderous reach of that policy of hate extended across Europe into the countries occupied by or allied with Germany.

Defining the Holocaust

Persecutions from the Past

Throughout history, European Jews were blamed when times were bad or other people felt hostile and needed a target. One important fact made the Holocaust different from past persecutions. During earlier persecutions, some Jews had a hope of surviving. During the Holocaust, they were not meant to survive.

Raul Hilberg, a historian who wrote about the Holocaust, summed up their persecutors' attitudes toward Jews at different periods in history.

In early Christian times, Christians told the Jews, **"You have no right to live among us as Jews."** This meant, "Convert to Christianity."

In the fifteenth century, European rulers confined Jews in ghettos and said, **"You have no right to live among us."** In other words, "You must live apart in the ghetto."

During the Holocaust, the Nazis said to the Jews, **"You have no right to live."**

Two Definitions

To understand the events Anne Frank describes in her diary, readers must first learn about the Holocaust. The Holocaust took place from 1933 to 1945 while the National Socialist (Nazi) Party, led by Adolf Hitler, controlled first Germany and then much of Europe. Those years of horror are referred to as the Third Reich.

This is how the United States Holocaust Memorial Council defines the Holocaust:

> The Holocaust was the systematic, bureaucratic annihilation of six million Jews by the Nazi regime and their collaborators as a central act of state during World War II. Although Jews were the primary victims, up to one half million Gypsies and at least 250,000 mentally or physically disabled persons were also victims of genocide. As Nazi tyranny spread across Europe from 1933 to 1945, millions of other innocent people were persecuted and often murdered. In addition, thousands of dissidents such as communists, socialists, trade unionists, Jehovah's Witnesses, and homosexuals were persecuted for their beliefs and behavior. Many of them died as a result of maltreatment.

Here is a simplified definition.

Under the Nazis, the goal of the German government was to kill all the Jewish people in Europe in a step-by-step plan carried out by government workers. Other people whom the Nazis considered unworthy were also marked for death.

Glossary

annihilation Complete destruction.

anti-Semitism Anti-Jewish actions, sentiments, or statements. (See A Brief History of Anti-Semitism on page 23.)

bureaucratic Originating in a government office; bureaucrats rigidly follow rules, forms, and routines.

central act of state A major government policy to which the resources and energies of a country are directed; a policy with wide-ranging national and international consequences.

expropriate To transfer ownership from another person to oneself.

genocide The deliberate killing of an entire group of people.

ghetto The section of many European cities in which Jews had traditionally been confined from the Middle Ages through the early 1880s. By the 1930s when Hitler came to power, Jewish ghettos in Europe were a thing of the past. They were started again by the Nazis and their followers.

persecute To oppress by harassing and torturing.

systematic Carried out in a step-by-step manner.

❖ Resource Pages

How the Holocaust Progressed (pages 27–28)

The Night of Broken Glass

"NAZIS SMASH, LOOT AND BURN JEWISH SHOPS AND TEMPLES," screamed the headline on the front page of *The New York Times* on November 11, 1938. *Kristallnacht* (KRIS-tal-nakht; "night of broken glass") took place in Germany and Austria on November 9 and 10, 1938. (Earlier that year, Austria had been taken over by Germany.)

The night was filled with a "mass frenzy of destruction," wrote one historian. The destruction of Jewish-owned property may have seemed like random acts of terrifying vandalism. It wasn't. *Kristallnacht* was actually a carefully planned, coordinated attack. It was ordered by Josef Goebbels, the Nazis' chief of propaganda. He used as his excuse the murder of a German diplomat in Paris. The diplomat was killed on November 8 by a Jewish teenager enraged by the expulsion from Germany of his family.

During *Kristallnacht*, synagogues were set on fire or destroyed completely. Mobs attacked Jewish shops and homes, smashing windows and looting the contents. Jews were taunted, beaten, and humiliated in the streets and in their homes. Many Jewish people died. *Kristallnacht* was used as an excuse to round up Jews who had been singled out for arrest earlier. More than 30,000 were taken to concentration camps at Dachau, Buchenwald, and Sachsenhausen. The arrest lists had been drawn up in advance. The camps had been made larger in preparation.

In response to the abuses of *Kristallnacht*, the governments of the United States and England presented formal diplomatic protests. They had little effect. After *Kristallnacht* thousands of Jews left Germany. Many more wanted to leave, but they could not find a country that would take them in.

Passersby seem unconcerned by the trashing of a Jewish-owned shop.

How the Holocaust Progressed

Raul Hilberg has done much research and writing about the killing of Jews during the Holocaust. In his book *The Destruction of the European Jews*, he describes the step-by-step process as four "legalized" stages. The steps are Definition, Expropriation, Concentration, and Annihilation. Hilberg calls them "legal" because the German legislature made them laws. To us they seem not only unlawful but immoral.

The existence of one stage did not mean the next had to follow. Each stage left people with choices. At any time, bureaucrats, government officials, Nazi Party members, and ordinary citizens could have chosen not to cooperate with the "laws."

Early 1930s. First Stage: Definition

In the definition stage, the Nazis defined a Jew based on irrational pseudo-scientific beliefs. This stage included requiring Jews to register for identity cards and separating Jews from others by visible symbols. Jewish people were forced to place the label "Jew" on their clothing, passports, or businesses. Later, laws required that a yellow star be sewn to the clothing of Jewish people.

Late 1930s. Second Stage: Expropriation

During the second stage, the property and livelihood of Jews were taken away (expropriated). Laws forbade Jews from holding certain jobs, living in certain places, owning businesses, or having bank accounts. Because Jews had already been identified in the first stage, it was easy to enforce the new laws against them.

August 1944: People being deported were forced onto packed cattle cars.

From early 1930s, intensified after 1939. Third Stage: Concentration

During this stage, German Jewish students were not allowed to attend school. German Jews' travel was restricted. They were not supposed to own phones, cameras, radios, or pets. This helped set Jews even farther apart from non-Jews. In Poland in 1939, Jews were moved from the countryside to cities. There they were crowded into walled sections set aside as ghettos. In the ghettos, many Jews worked as slave laborers, surviving on limited supplies of food, shelter, and heat. Life in the ghetto was slow death.

From 1941 in parts of Eastern Europe; intensified after 1942.
Fourth Stage: Annihilation

In this final stage, the Nazis organized and carried out large-scale killing of Jews and others—people who disagreed with or spoke out or acted against the Nazis; members of banned political parties such as Communists or Social Democrats; Jehovah's Witnesses and members of many religious groups; Gypsies; homosexuals; blacks; and people with mental and physical disabilities. Some were shot or gassed by mobile killing units in parts of Russia, Latvia, and Lithuania. In the rest of Europe, the victims were transported to killing centers. There, just before people were killed, one last "expropriation" took place. The personal property taken from people at killing centers included toys, clothing, shoes, eyeglasses, and women's hair.

It is very important to understand that none of these stages were inevitable. People could decide whether or not to enforce the laws and whether or not to comply with them. But people who resisted were usually imprisoned or executed. The Nazis singled out Jews for death, but they were not the regime's only targets. Others imprisoned and murdered included anyone who disagreed with or spoke out or acted against the Nazis.

Talk It Over

1. What do you think it takes for a person to defy a law he or she feels is unjust?

2. Have you ever spoken out against a policy or plan? What were the consequences?

3. Can you think of times in American history when to speak out was a matter of life and death? What were the circumstances? (In the 1960s, for example, civil rights activists were murdered. But, though local authorities may not have protected them, the federal government did finally step in. No national policy of annihilation existed as it did in Nazi Germany.)

Adapted from *The Destruction of the European Jews* by Raul Hilberg, Franklin Watts, 1973.

Teaching the Diary of Anne Frank Scholastic Professional Books

Voyage of the *St. Louis*

After *Kristallnacht* in November 1938, more and more Jews tried to leave Germany and Austria. But they found that almost every country in the world was closed to them. In July 1938, representatives from 32 countries had met in Evian, France, to discuss policies on Jewish people fleeing Nazi terror. Only the tiny Dominican Republic, in the Caribbean Sea, offered to take in large numbers of Jewish refugees. The United States was among the nations that refused.

The fate of the passengers on the *St. Louis* shows how indifferent the world was to the plight of Jews. In May 1939, more than 900 Jewish people set sail from Germany on the *St. Louis*, a Hamburg-America line ship. They believed they were on their way to safety. But they were the victims of a cruel deception. The Germans had told the refugees that Cuba agreed to take them in, but that was a lie. The Germans knew that the Cuban government would refuse to allow the Jews to land.

When the *St. Louis* reached Cuba, only 30 passengers were allowed to come ashore. Then, for more than a month, the *St. Louis* roamed the seas. Its desperate passengers tried to find a country that would admit them. At last, England, Holland, Belgium, and France agreed to take some of the refugees.

Only the passengers who went to England were relatively safe. The rest returned to Germany, where they were sent to concentration camps. And after the Germans invaded Holland, Belgium, and France in 1940, the fate of the Jewish people in those nations was sealed as well.

Two passengers gaze through a porthole of the St. Louis.

Introducing Anne Frank

Anne Frank

German Jewish soldier of
World War I

What do your students know about Anne Frank and events in Europe during World War II? Do students have any questions? Share the following information.

The experiences of Anne Frank's family were much like those of many European Jews during the first half of the twentieth century. Otto and Edith Frank were both from Jewish families that considered themselves assimilated; that is, they saw themselves as Germans and believed that other people saw—and accepted—them as Germans, too. Otto and his brother had served in the German army in World War I. When Otto and Edith married, they settled in Frankfurt am Main, where their daughters were born, Margot in 1926 and Anne in 1929. But after Hitler came to power and restricted and persecuted Jews, the Franks no longer felt welcome in Germany. They moved to the Netherlands, where many German Jews had found acceptance. There they decided to bring up their children (Anne, age four, and Margot, age seven, at the time they moved).

The Franks lived comfortably in Amsterdam from 1934 until 1940, when the Netherlands fell under Nazi control. Otto Frank's two businesses prospered; the family, especially Anne, made friends. Even after the German occupation of the Netherlands, as Anne's diary shows, the life of the children, at least, seemed fairly normal. Despite a government-imposed curfew, change of schools (Anne went from the Montessori School to the Jewish Lyceum), and identification (the yellow star), Anne and her friends were able to enjoy Ping-Pong, ice cream, and parties. But the restrictions became more intense, and the "terrible nets" of destruction, carefully devised by Nazi bureaucrats in Germany, were tightening around them.

Talk about the events on the time line, using the maps as reference. Review the years up to 1942 when the Frank family went into hiding. The time line will help you obtain a more complete picture as students read the diary and work on related activities in this section of the guide.

Anne with her class at the Montessori school

The four maps on The Expansion of Germany Resource Pages show Germany at four crucial stages.

- The map for 1933, the year Hitler came to power, shows Germany's borders as defined by the Treaty of Versailles at the end of World War I.

- The map for 1939, the year World War II began, shows the extent to which the Third Reich had already expanded beyond those borders.

- The 1942 map shows the extent of the Third Reich at the peak of its power, as well as those parts of Europe that were occupied by or allied with Germany.

- The 1945 map shows a divided Germany inside borders defined by the Allies at the end of World War II.

For 1939 and 1942, have students connect events on the time line with Germany's territorial expansion.

❖ Resource Pages

A Frank Family Album

Photographs of the Frank family before going into hiding.

Anne Frank, with her mother Edith, early 1930s

Margot Frank, early 1930s

Anne Frank (right), with Sanne Ledermann and Eva Goldberg, 1936

Anne Frank, with her sister Margot and father Otto, 1930

Anne Frank at school, 1940

Teaching the Diary of Anne Frank   Scholastic Professional Books

Time Line: Anne Frank's World—1914–1945

The complete time line is five pages. To assemble, align the time line at the edge of each page and tape in place.

Children use banknotes as building blocks during the inflation crisis.

German soldiers rest after a World War I battle.

Margot and Anne, 1933

1914–1918

World Events
World War I

The Frank Family
Otto Frank serves in the German Army during World War I.

1919–1924

World Events
Turmoil in Germany following the Treaty of Versailles. Inflation causes financial hardships and contributes to people's loss of faith in the government. Communists and National Socialists propose radical solutions including the overthrow of the democratic government.

The Frank Family
Otto Frank, a banker, marries Edith Hollander, from Aachen, Germany, near the Dutch border. They settle in Frankfurt am Main, Germany.

1924–September 1929

World Events
German economy improves, thanks to foreign aid; Communist and National Socialist parties lose influence.

The Frank Family
The Franks' two daughters are born—Margot in 1926, and Annelies Marie, called Anne, in 1929.

Hitler (left) and Hermann Goering

World Events

The crash of the New York stock market plunges the world into an economic depression. Many of the German bankers who lose money through investments in the United States are Jewish.

World Events

Adolf Hitler is voted into power and becomes chancellor of Germany. The National Socialist (Nazi) Party is legally designated the only political party in Germany. Hitler blames Jews for the world's economic ills. Rioting occurs against German Jews. Hitler decrees emergency powers suspending freedom of speech, press, and the right to assemble. Political opponents are arrested and sent to Dachau, the first concentration camp opened in Germany. All Jews in civil service jobs are fired. Jewish professors are fired from universities. Jews are barred from working in the theater, movies, arts, court system, press, and education, and as doctors and dentists. Books by Jews and opponents of the Nazis are burned. Anti-Semitism becomes accepted law and practice.

World Events

Germany passes more anti-Jewish legislation. Jews lose their German citizenship as well as the right to vote and to hold elected office. Jews cannot serve in the German army. Non-Jewish Germans cannot marry Jews.

Germans are not permitted to work in Jewish homes. Polish Jews start a general strike against anti-Semitism. In preparation for the 1936 Olympics, held in Germany that year, anti-Semitic signs are removed from most public places. In 1936 Germany occupies the Rhineland, an area taken away from Germany after World War I.

▲ **October 1929–January 1933** ▲ **1933–1934** ▲ **1935–1937** ▲

The Frank Family

Otto Frank loses his job. His parents and many other wealthy Germans lose their fortunes. Dissatisfaction and suffering lead people to turn again to Communist and National Socialist parties.

The Frank Family

The Franks move to Amsterdam, the Netherlands.

The Frank Family

The Franks settle into life in the Netherlands. Anne and Margot make friends; Anne attends a Montessori school. *(see photo below)*

World Events

Buchenwald concentration camp opens. In March, Austria is annexed to the Third Reich. In July, representatives from 32 countries meet in Evian, France, to discuss policies on Jewish refugees from Nazi terror. Except for the tiny Dominican Republic, no countries offer to take large numbers of Jewish refugees. In September, at Munich, Britain and France agree to Hitler's plan to annex part of Czechoslovakia. "Aryanization" (taking over the property of German Jews) begins. In November, a night of anti-Jewish violence, *Kristallnacht*, sweeps through Germany and Austria, fueled by the Nazis. One thousand Jews are killed and 30,000 Jews are arrested and sent to concentration camps. German Jews are fined the equivalent of $400 million. All Jewish property must be registered. Jews are not allowed to have radios, telephones, or pets. They are forbidden to go to barbers or beauty shops and cannot buy rationed food. All Jewish children are expelled from public schools. Passports of Jews are marked with the letter **J.**

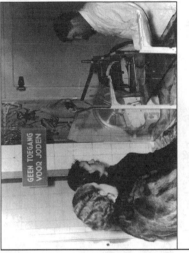

The sign says that the line is for Jewish shoppers.

World Events

In March, the Germans occupy Czechoslovakia. In June, 900 Jewish refugees return to Europe after being refused entry by Cuba and the United States. In August, Hitler signs a nonaggression pact with the Soviet Union, clearing the way for the invasion of Poland without Soviet interference. World War II begins on September 1 with Germany's invasion of Poland. On September 3, Britain and France declare war on Germany. Most of Poland falls under Nazi rule. Reinhard Heydrich, head of the security police, orders Jews in Poland to move into ghettos. Polish Jews are ordered to wear armbands with yellow Star of David.

1938

The Frank Family

Otto Frank establishes a second company in Amsterdam.

Anne and Margot

1939

The Frank Family

Life in Germany becomes intolerable for Grandmother Hollander, Edith Frank's mother. She moves to Amsterdam to live with the Franks.

World Events

In April, Germany invades Denmark and southern Norway. A concentration camp is set up at Auschwitz in Poland. In May, Holland, Belgium, and France fall. In November, the Warsaw ghetto in Poland is sealed off from the rest of Warsaw. In December, historian Emmanuel Ringelblum and others set up secret archives in the Warsaw ghetto.

The Netherlands

In May, the German army invades and occupies the Netherlands. The Dutch royal family and cabinet ministers flee to England, where they set up the Dutch government-in-exile.

World Events

In March, Germany invades North Africa; in April, Yugoslavia and Greece; in June, Russia. Massacre of Jews by mobile killing units takes place in areas of Russia and Eastern Europe under German control. On December 7, after the Japanese bomb U.S. naval ships in Pearl Harbor, Hawaii, the United States declares war on Japan and Germany. Germany declares war on the United States. In December, Chelmno, the first killing center, opens in Poland.

The Netherlands

All Dutch citizens are given an identity card. Jews' cards are marked **J.** Jewish children can no longer attend the school of their choice. Jews lose control over their assets; bank accounts and real estate holdings are blocked.

World Events

In January, at the Wannsee Conference, leading Nazis record details of their plan for the final solution—killing 14,000,000 European Jews (their estimate). Killing centers open at Sobibor, Belzic, and Treblinka. Deportation and killings begin. Between July and September, 300,000 Jews are taken from the Warsaw ghetto to Treblinka. The Jewish combat organization is established in Poland and attacks German soldiers. In November, the British defeat the Germans in North Africa.

The Netherlands

Starting in May, all Jews in the Netherlands above the age of six have to wear a yellow Star of David with the word *Jood* (Jew) on it. In July, more than 1,000 young Jews are called up for "labor in the east" and are transported to Poland.

The Frank Family

Otto Frank's company moves to number 263 on the Prinsengracht Canal. All Jewish civil servants in the Netherlands are fired.

The center house is where the Franks hid.

The Frank Family

Otto Frank transfers ownership of his company to his non-Jewish colleagues because Jews are no longer allowed to own companies. Anne and Margot transfer to a Jewish school because Jews are no longer allowed to attend school with other Dutch children.

The Frank Family

Anne receives a diary on June 12, her thirteenth birthday. On July 5, Margot receives a notice to report for a "labor transport." On July 6, the Franks go into hiding, joined a few days later by the three Van Daans and in November by Alfred Dussel.

The suffering was widespread.

Many Dutch people went hungry during the war.

1943

World Events
Jewish armed resistance begins in the Warsaw ghetto. Hundreds of underground fighters leave the Vilna ghetto for the forests. Italy declares war on Germany.

The Netherlands
Large deportations of Jews leave the Netherlands bound for killing centers in Poland.

The Frank Family
In hiding, Anne observes the people around her, studies, writes stories, and makes entries in her diary.

1944

World Events
In March, the German army invades Hungary; 500,000 Jews are deported from Hungary to Auschwitz. On June 6, the Allies land in Normandy on the French coast to begin their push toward Germany from the west as the Soviet armies push from the east.

The Netherlands
Nazis intensify their searches for Jews in hiding. Dutch men are rounded up and sent to work in Germany. Deliberate limitations on food and fuel imposed by the Nazis in the winter of 1944–1945 result in starvation in Dutch cities.

The Frank Family
On August 4, the hiding place is discovered and all eight people are arrested. They are sent first to Westerbork, a transit camp in the Netherlands, and then to Auschwitz in Poland. In October, Anne and Margot are taken to Bergen-Belsen.

1945

World Events
On January 26, the Russians liberate Auschwitz. On April 30, Hitler commits suicide. On May 8, Germany surrenders and World War II ends.

The Netherlands
The Netherlands is liberated in May. Of the Jews in the Netherlands before the war, three out of four are dead by its end.

The Frank Family
On January 5, Edith Frank dies in Auschwitz. On January 26, Otto Frank is liberated from Auschwitz by the Russians; it takes him until June to reach Amsterdam. In March, Margot and Anne die in Bergen-Belsen, probably of typhus, a few weeks before the camp is liberated by British troops. On May 5, Peter Van Daan dies in Mauthausen concentration camp. Of the eight people who hid in the Secret Annexe, only Otto Frank survives the war.

Maps: The Expansion of Germany

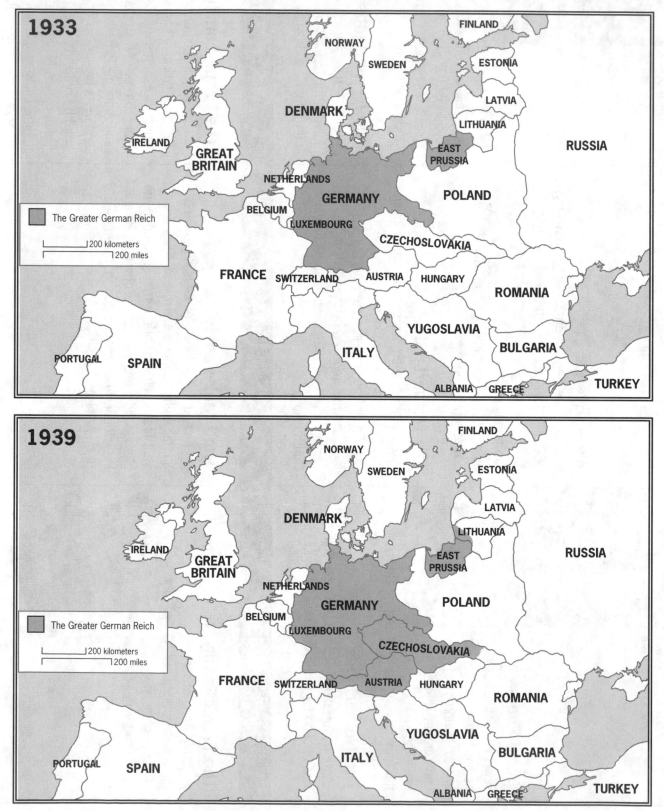

1933

FINLAND
NORWAY
SWEDEN
ESTONIA
DENMARK
LATVIA
LITHUANIA
IRELAND
EAST PRUSSIA
RUSSIA
GREAT BRITAIN
NETHERLANDS
GERMANY
POLAND
BELGIUM
LUXEMBOURG
CZECHOSLOVAKIA
FRANCE
SWITZERLAND
AUSTRIA
HUNGARY
ROMANIA
YUGOSLAVIA
BULGARIA
PORTUGAL
SPAIN
ITALY
TURKEY
ALBANIA
GREECE

The Greater German Reich

200 kilometers
200 miles

1939

FINLAND
NORWAY
SWEDEN
ESTONIA
DENMARK
LATVIA
LITHUANIA
IRELAND
EAST PRUSSIA
RUSSIA
GREAT BRITAIN
NETHERLANDS
GERMANY
POLAND
BELGIUM
LUXEMBOURG
CZECHOSLOVAKIA
FRANCE
SWITZERLAND
AUSTRIA
HUNGARY
ROMANIA
YUGOSLAVIA
BULGARIA
PORTUGAL
SPAIN
ITALY
TURKEY
ALBANIA
GREECE

The Greater German Reich

200 kilometers
200 miles

Maps: The Expansion of Germany

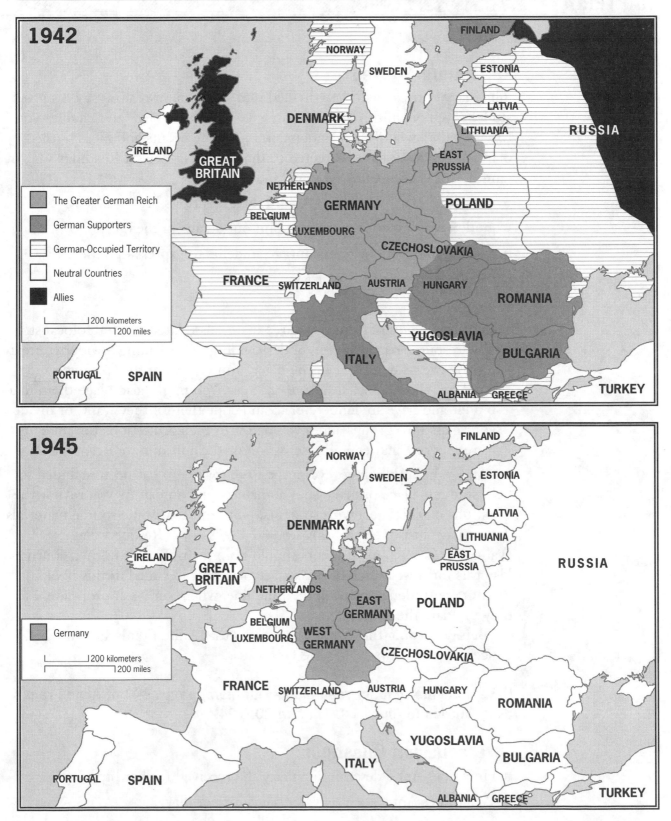

1942

Legend:
- The Greater German Reich
- German Supporters
- German-Occupied Territory
- Neutral Countries
- Allies

200 kilometers
200 miles

NORWAY · SWEDEN · FINLAND · ESTONIA · LATVIA · LITHUANIA · RUSSIA · DENMARK · EAST PRUSSIA · IRELAND · GREAT BRITAIN · NETHERLANDS · GERMANY · POLAND · BELGIUM · LUXEMBOURG · CZECHOSLOVAKIA · FRANCE · SWITZERLAND · AUSTRIA · HUNGARY · ROMANIA · YUGOSLAVIA · BULGARIA · ITALY · PORTUGAL · SPAIN · ALBANIA · GREECE · TURKEY

1945

Legend:
- Germany

200 kilometers
200 miles

NORWAY · SWEDEN · FINLAND · ESTONIA · LATVIA · LITHUANIA · RUSSIA · DENMARK · EAST PRUSSIA · IRELAND · GREAT BRITAIN · NETHERLANDS · EAST GERMANY · WEST GERMANY · POLAND · BELGIUM · LUXEMBOURG · CZECHOSLOVAKIA · FRANCE · SWITZERLAND · AUSTRIA · HUNGARY · ROMANIA · YUGOSLAVIA · BULGARIA · ITALY · PORTUGAL · SPAIN · ALBANIA · GREECE · TURKEY

Understanding the Diary

CHAPTER 4

❖ Getting Started

The diary entries have been divided into six parts, or readings. This gives students opportunities to reflect on what they have read, and enables you to assess the level of their understanding of the events and ideas in the diary. The questions are directed to the students. The six Readings vary in length. For each reading, you will find

- notes that clarify incidents Anne Frank mentions in her diary.

- guided reading questions that point out details in the diary.

- discussion questions to encourage students to express opinions.

- ideas for the response journal.

- projects.

- Resource Pages of primary source materials related to the Holocaust. The resource pages deepen understanding by providing a wider context for the events described in the diary. You may want to reproduce and hand out all or selected Resource Pages. You might also place them in a binder and have students refer to and copy them if they want, or divide your class into groups and give one set to each. Questions for students to reflect on, answer, and discuss follow the appropriate Resource Pages.

An Evaluating Sources Resource Page (page 46) has been included to help students place primary-source material in context. As you review the questions on this sheet with students, point out that some source materials do not have just one author. After you discuss each Resource Page, evaluate it as a group. Students should note their answers in their journals. Use this form with each of the source materials included in this book. Encourage students to check the time line, whenever it's appropriate, as they evaluate the sources.

Before reading the diary, tell students that Anne Frank died in a Nazi concentration camp during the Holocaust.

Have students read, or read aloud with them, pages 1–3 of Anne Frank's diary entries for June 14, 15, and 20, 1942.

❖ Discussion Questions

- How does Anne describe the diary she received for her birthday?

- What does Anne say about her plans for her diary?

■ How many of you regularly keep a diary in which you record daily events, your thoughts and feelings, or both?

❖ Keeping Response Journals

Tell students something like this:

> We will each be keeping response journals as we read *The Diary of a Young Girl* and the primary-source materials that are part of this unit. Keeping journals will help us to better understand the materials and to deal with upsetting information. Writing about a topic helps us organize our thoughts and think of questions. Unlike personal diaries, which are usually private, the response journals are to be shared. In them we can record our feelings and reactions as we try to understand this difficult subject.
>
> I, too, will be keeping a journal and will share it with you. I will collect, read, and comment on your journals from time to time. Students who read my journal may comment on a separate sheet of paper. Please sign your names to your comments.
>
> As we read the diary and the other materials, take time to reflect in your journals about what we are reading or to respond to your earlier entries. I will make a schedule of times to collect and review your journals and to share my entries with you. Here are some suggestions for keeping a response journal.

❖ Resource Page

Keeping a Response Journal (page 42)

BACKGROUND

Why You Should Keep a Response Journal and Share It with Students

By joining students in writing and sharing the journal assignments, you can:

model an effective learning technique.

identify and understand your own reactions to the diary and to the primary-source materials.

empathize with reluctant writers.

experience the vulnerability students feel when their journals are read by you.

deepen your knowledge of the Holocaust by sharing your feelings of grief and outrage with students.

stimulate students' interest in the assignments.

learn from students' comments on your ideas.

Keeping a Response Journal

Here are some suggestions as you begin your response journal.

❖ Format

- Use a spiral-bound notebook.
- Write your name on the first page and on the cover.
- Use right-hand pages for first reactions and left-hand pages for your later comments.
- Date each entry.
- Write every day and review the entries once a week to make comments. Since you'll be adding information as you go through the unit, you may find that your opinions have changed. It will be interesting to look back and see our process of understanding.

❖ Responding to Anne Frank's Diary in Your Journal

Feel free to expand on reading assignments with your own reflections on what you read. Ideas for journal entries will be suggested for each assigned reading. Write the date and page number of each of the diary entries you comment on. Sometimes you may want to do drawings or write poetry as well as write personal statements.

First Journal Assignment:
As a starting point, write about a time you stood up for something you thought was right or about a time you looked the other way. Then comment on this question posed by the author of *Terrible Things* in her introduction: "If everyone had stood together at the first sign of evil would [the Holocaust] have happened?"

Teaching the Diary of Anne Frank Scholastic Professional Books

Reading 1

(pages 1–21 in Bantam paperback, 1993)

Sunday, June 14, 1942–Saturday, July 11, 1942

Diary entry written June 1942; notes added in September 1942

❖ Summary

These entries introduce the reader to Anne and her family. They cover the time between Anne's thirteenth birthday, the day she receives her diary, and the day she and her family go into hiding.

❖ Notes on the Diary

Share this information with students.

June 20, 24; July 3, 5, 1942: References to anti-Jewish laws

See Resource Page, Laws Against the Jewish People, page 48.

July 8: Margot receives a call-up notice.

Call-ups like the one Margot received usually said, "report for resettlement for labor in the east." But they were really death notices. Large-scale deportations from Holland started in July 1942. The Jews were taken to killing centers in Poland—Sobibor or Auschwitz—where thousands were immediately put to death and others slowly died from hunger or disease. About 140,000 Jews lived in the Netherlands. About 115,000 Jews were deported. Three out of four of all Dutch Jews were killed.

Anne writes of this 1942 photograph: "This photograph is horrible, and I look absolutely nothing like it." The note on the next page is dated September 10, 1942.

July 5, 8, 1942: Going into hiding

The Dutch word for going underground is *onderduiker:* literally, one who dives under. In the flat Dutch countryside it was impossible to hide and fight from the cover of thick woods as many Jews in Eastern Europe did. The Jews of the Netherlands had to hide in cities or the countryside. Like the Franks, they were hidden by other people. Of 25,000 who tried to evade arrest and deportation in this way, 18,000 were saved. This was 25 percent of the total Jewish population; it is a tribute to the bravery of the non-Jewish Dutch people involved.

❖ Guided Reading Questions

As they read the diary entries, have students consider these questions and write their answers in their journals.

1. What was Anne's life like before she went into hiding?

2. How did anti-Jewish laws restrict Anne and her friends?

3. How and why did Anne's life change on July 6, 1942?

❖ Discussion Questions

- What does the "chatterbox" incident tell you about the kind of person Anne was (June 21, 1942)? Find some other examples that reveal her distinctive personality.

- How does Anne's reaction to the family's hiding place differ from Margot's and Mrs. Frank's (July 9–11, 1942)?

- How does Anne make herself feel at home in the hiding place? What does this tell you about her (July 11, 1942)?

❖ Response Journal Ideas

- What do these statements from the diary mean to you?

   "Paper is more patient than man" (June 20, 1942).

   "It is not the Dutch people's fault that we are having such a miserable time" (June 24, 1942).

   "I can't tell you how oppressive it is *never* to be able to go outdoors" (July 11, 1942).

- In occupied countries like the Netherlands, the Nazis imposed the same type of laws against the Jews as they had in Germany. In her diary, Anne mentions some of the restrictions she and her friends put up with (June 20, June 24, and July 5, 1942). List them in your journal. Describe how one or more of these restrictions might affect you.

❖ Project

Describing how she packed to go into hiding, Anne says, "The first thing I put in was this diary, then hair curlers, handkerchiefs, schoolbooks, a comb, old letters; I put in the craziest things. . . . But I'm not sorry, memories mean more to me than dresses" (July 8, 1942).

   What do the things she packed tell you about Anne? Bring into class something that holds memories for you. Explain why it is meaningful. In your journal describe the importance of your memories and how you hold on to them.

❖ Resource Pages

Evaluating Sources (page 46)

Discrimination Against the Jewish People (page 47)

Laws Against the Jewish People (page 48)

Evaluating Sources

Use this page to help you evaluate documents relating to the Holocaust.

What is the title of the document?

Who do you think wrote the document?

What language was it originally written in?

Who is the document's intended audience?

What is the date of the document? If it was written during World War II, what was happening in Europe at the time?

How does the document help you understand Anne Frank's diary or her life?

If you could speak to the document's writer, what would you say?

Teaching the Diary of Anne Frank   Scholastic Professional Books

Discrimination Against the Jewish People

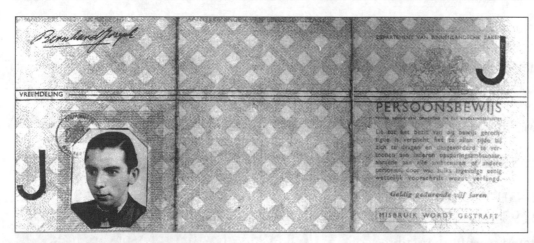

A **J** marked the identity cards of Jewish people, such as this Dutch man.

Jewish people in the Netherlands were forced to wear Stars of David on their clothing. In the center was the word Jew.

A sign marks the Jewish section of Amsterdam, the Netherlands.

Talk It Over

1. *Jood* is the Dutch word for Jew. Anne mentions wearing a yellow star when her family walks to their hiding place (July 9, 1942). Why do you think the Nazis forced Jews to identify themselves by wearing a yellow star? Why were Jews forbidden to enter public parks?

2. How do the star and the sign illustrate the first—the definition—stage of the Holocaust?

3. What are some identifying symbols that people wear today because they want to?

4. How do those voluntary actions differ from laws requiring Jews to wear yellow stars?

Teaching the Diary of Anne Frank Scholastic Professional Books

Laws Against the Jewish People

When Hitler became dictator in 1933, his Nazi legislature began to pass laws defining *Jew* and restricting where Jews could work. As a result of these laws, many people, Jews and non-Jews, left Germany in protest and in fear. Otto and Edith Frank left Germany for the Netherlands. In 1935, Hitler's National Socialist (Nazi) government passed laws declaring that Jews were no longer German citizens. By the time the Germans occupied the Netherlands in 1940, Jewish people had few places to which they could flee.

—REICH CITIZENSHIP LAW, SEPTEMBER 15, 1935

§ 2. (1) A Reich citizen is only that subject of German or kindred blood who proves by his conduct that he is willing and suited loyally to serve the German people and the Reich.

—FIRST DECREE TO REICH CITIZENSHIP LAW, NOVEMBER 14, 1935

§ 3. Only a Reich citizen, as bearer of full political rights, can exercise the right to vote on political matters, or hold public office.

§ 4. (1) A Jew cannot be a Reich citizen. He is not entitled to the right to vote on political matters; he cannot hold public office.

Other Anti-Jewish Laws in Germany

1933 Jewish professors are fired from universities.

1935 Jews may no longer serve in the German army.

1935 Jews and Aryans (Hitler's distorted idea of a German "race") may not marry each other.

1938 All Jewish property must be registered. Passports of Jews are marked with **J**.

1939 Polish Jews are ordered to wear armbands with yellow Star of David.

Talk It Over

1. What is citizenship?

2. How do you think these laws affected Jews in Germany in 1935?

3. How are other laws in Germany similar to the restrictions mentioned by Anne Frank on June 20, June 24, and July 5, 1942?

4. Why did people put up with these restrictive laws?

5. How do these laws illustrate the definition stage of the Holocaust?

6. Research how a person becomes a U.S. citizen. Can U.S. citizenship be taken away? Visit your local library to find newspaper reports of people who have been deported from the United States or who have had their citizenship taken away. What were the reasons? How is this the same as or different from what happened in Europe in the 1940s?

Teaching the Diary of Anne Frank Scholastic Professional Books

Reading 2

Friday, August 14, 1942–Monday, November 9, 1942

❖ Summary

These entries describe Anne's life in hiding up to the arrival of Alfred Dussel, the eighth person in the Secret Annexe. Many of the entries focus on Anne's feelings about other people, objective descriptions of the Secret Annexe, subjective descriptions of its inhabitants, how she spends her days in hiding, and her reactions to events in the world outside.

❖ Notes on the Diary

Share this information with students.

July 11, 1942: Listening to the BBC

The Nazis controlled all the news printed or broadcast in Germany and occupied Europe. But by tuning their radios to the BBC (the British Broadcasting Corporation), people could get news reports from England. The BBC news broadcasts kept up the morale of countless thousands of secret listeners all over Europe. They listened in secret because access to the BBC was strictly forbidden by the Nazis. (That's why Anne expresses nervousness when the adults listen to broadcasts in hiding.) The penalties for listening to an unauthorized station were severe. Coded messages to resistance groups were regularly broadcast on the BBC.

Next to the photograph she added to her diary in October 1942, Anne commented, "This is a photograph of me as I wish I looked all the time. Then I might still have a chance of getting to Hollywood. But at present, I'm afraid, I usually look quite different."

September 21, 1942: The Dutch royal family in England

Queen Wilhelmina, with her family and cabinet ministers, escaped to England three days after the Germans invaded the Netherlands in May 1940. The queen made frequent radio broadcasts to rally her Dutch subjects. She came to symbolize the spirit of Dutch independence and Dutch values. Churchill admiringly referred to her as "the bravest man in England."

October 9, 29, 1942: German treatment of Dutch Jews; the Van Daans' furniture

Under the Nazis, Dutch Jews were subjected to the same restrictions as Jews in Germany. But in the Netherlands the process took place in just over two years—from May 1940 when the Germans occupied the Netherlands to July 1942 when the first deportations began. In that time,

Nazis humiliated elderly Jewish men by forcing them to clean streets with toothbrushes.

most Jews were deprived of their businesses and property. They were forced to identify themselves—first by a **J** on their identity cards and then by a yellow star on their clothing—and forced to move into three ghetto areas of Amsterdam. Contact between Jews and non-Jews was also regulated. In 1941, Jewish students could no longer attend school with other Dutch children. These measures, designed to isolate the Jews, were effective—some Dutch people began to fear associating with Jews. Other Dutch people—both Jews and non-Jews—fought back against the Germans and their collaborators, the Dutch Nazi Party. Saboteurs committed acts of destruction. People who were caught committing sabotage or resisting in other ways were usually tortured and executed.

When deportations began, the property that Jews left behind—referred to as "ownerless" by the Germans in charge of collecting it—was removed by a Dutch moving company under contract to the German authorities. The furniture was taken to Germany where it was either sold or distributed to people whose homes had been bombed.

November 9, 1942: British landing in North Africa

In November 1942, U.S. and British forces under General Dwight D. Eisenhower landed in North Africa. By May, the German and Italian forces surrendered. This was the first major Allied blow against Germany.

SPIRITUAL RESISTANCE   Talk about this concept with students; it is a concept they will continually refer to as they look at the source materials in this book. Resistance during the Holocaust took many forms. We usually think of resistance as violent acts of sabotage or battles fought with guns (see the references from the diary). But disobeying orders, reading banned books, and helping Jews or others declared unacceptable by the Nazis were also acts of resistance. Miep Gies and the other "helpers" who took care of the Franks in hiding were committing acts of resistance; so was Anne by writing in her diary. Spiritual resistance meant studying, learning, monitoring the progress of the war, recording information (diaries), telling the truth in the face of lies, maintaining hope and religious beliefs in the face of the complete disruption of life. In the context of the hate-filled years of the Holocaust, loving other people and acting on that love was as much an act of resistance as killing Nazis or blowing up railroad lines.

❖ Guided Reading Questions

As they read the diary entries, have students consider these questions and note their responses in their journals.

1. How did Anne and the other residents of the Secret Annexe spend their time during their first months in hiding?

2. How does Anne describe the Van Daan family? Give some examples of the details that make her writing about people lively and interesting.

❖ Discussion Questions

■ Anne writes: "It's extremely important to be able to write in code" (October 1, 1942). Why was writing in code so important for her? What code did Anne learn and how do you think it helped her?

■ What does Anne report about Jews in Holland who were not able to go into hiding? What does she mean when she says Hitler took away her "nationality" (October 9, 1942)?

■ What kind of help could people of the Netherlands offer the Jews?

BACKGROUND

Rescue in Denmark

About 8,000 Jewish people lived in Denmark when it surrendered to the Germans in 1940. Until 1943 there were few restrictions on any of the Danes—Christians or Jews. Then the noose tightened. The Nazis ordered the deportation of the Jews of Denmark. But the deportation did not go as planned: A German official warned a member of the Danish resistance, who passed the message on to leaders of the Jewish community. A nationwide effort to save the Jews immediately swung into action.

The Danish resistance and thousands of ordinary Danes helped set up a rescue effort. By boat, they transported 6,000 Jews, 1,300 part-Jews, and 680 non-Jewish family members to neutral Sweden at the end of September and the beginning of October 1943. (Although it was neutral, Sweden was accepting Jews and others fleeing the Nazis.)

In the end, about 500 Danish Jews were deported to Theresienstadt ghetto in the Protectorate of Bohemia and Moravia (formerly Czechoslovakia). Theresienstadt was a transit camp, deporting people regularly to Auschwitz. But because of the tireless efforts of the Danish Red Cross and other Danes, 423 Danish Jews survived Theresienstadt.

❖ Response Journal Ideas

- Describe a family member or a close friend as objectively as possible. Then try writing an objective description of yourself.

- Describe a "perfect" day.

- Describe a time when you felt confined.

- On September 28, 1942, Anne writes: "You only really get to know people when you've had a jolly good row [argument] with them. Then and only then can you judge their true characters!" Give an example from your own experience that either supports or challenges Anne's statement.

- In her book *Anne Frank Remembered*, Miep Gies says, "I am not a hero. . . . My story is the story of very ordinary people during extraordinarily terrible times." Write about something ordinary people can do to prevent the "terrible times" from coming again.

- How does the example of what Danish people did show the power of sticking together?

❖ Projects

- Assign groups of students to explore what happened to Jews who wanted to leave Germany before 1939. One group could report on the ill-fated S.S. *St. Louis* (see page 29). A second group could investigate where other members of Otto Frank's family fled. (For a starting place, see the entry for June 20, 1942.) A third group could research the immigration policies of the United States in the late 1930s.

- On the floor of the classroom, approximate the area of the room Anne shared with Mr. Dussel (6 feet 6 inches by 16 feet 6 inches). Mark the boundaries with masking tape. Then have pairs of students spend some time in the space. Students can write about what it would feel like to share that small a space with someone else for a long period of time.

❖ Resource Pages

The Story of Oskar Schindler

Oskar Schindler (1908–1974), a German industrialist and Nazi Party member, rescued 1,300 Jews from concentration camps in Poland. First he hired them as laborers. Then he protected them from deportation to death camps. Other German industrialists treated their employees as consumable slave labor. Schindler provided food, clothing, shelter, and, when the Nazi killers were on his doorstep, life itself.

Oskar Schindler

His first factory in Krakow, Poland, produced enamelware pots and pans for the German army and other customers. When the threats to his Jewish workers intensified in Poland, he relocated to Czechoslovakia. There he set up a factory to which he moved his workers so he could better protect them. This factory produced weapon parts that were deliberately sabotaged so they could not be used. At the end of the war, his Jewish workers helped Schindler and his wife escape Czechoslovakia to avoid the Russian army.

Schindler was a complicated character. He used his reputation as a prosperous man of the world to effectively protect "his" Jews. With black market connections, he was able to bribe Nazi officials with liquor and expensive gifts. By using his image as a self-interested businessman, he accomplished the impossible—snatching more than 1,000 Jews from the jaws of the Nazi death machine.

In 1961, Oskar Schindler was declared a Righteous Gentile by Yad Vashem, the Israeli State Holocaust Memorial and Research Center. Oskar Schindler is immortalized in Steven Spielberg's 1993 film *Schindler's List* and in Thomas Keneally's novel of the same name.

Moment of Decision

by Miep Gies

This is an excerpt from *Anne Frank Remembered,* a book written in 1987 by Miep Gies, the woman who helped the Franks while they were in hiding. Here, Miep (MEEP) describes the day in the spring of 1942 when Otto Frank told her that he intended to go into hiding with his family and the Van Daans.

July 16, 1941: Miep on her wedding day

He locked eyes with me, his soft brown eyes looking deeply into mine with an almost piercing directness. "Miep," he began, "I have a secret to confide to you."

I listened silently.

"Miep," he said, "Edith, Margot, Anne and I are planning to go under—to go into hiding."

He let me take this in.

"We will go together with Van Daan and his wife and their son." Mr. Frank paused. "I'm sure you know the empty rooms where my pharmacist friend Lewin has been making his experiments?"

I told him I knew of these rooms but had never gone into them.

"That is where we will hide."

He paused for a moment.

"As you will be working on, as usual, right next to us, I need to know if you have any objections?"

I told him I did not.

He took a breath and asked, "Miep, are you willing to take on the responsibility of taking care of us while we are in hiding?"

"Of course," I answered.

There is a look between two people once or twice in a lifetime that cannot be described in words. That look passed between us. "Miep, for those who help Jews, the punishment is harsh; imprisonment, perhaps—"

I cut him off. "I said, 'Of course.' I meant it."

"Good. Only Koophuis [a business partner and friend] knows. Even Margot and Anne do not know yet. One by one I will ask the others. But only a few will know."

I asked no further questions. The less I knew, the less I could say in an interrogation. I knew when the time was right he would tell me who the others were, and everything else I would need to know. I felt no curiosity. I had given my word.

Talk It Over

1. Why did Otto Frank feel it was necessary to go into hiding with his family? What were the pros and cons of the Secret Annexe as a hiding place?

2. What do you think motivated people who hid the Franks and others? What risks did they run?

3. What did Otto Frank mean when he said to Miep, ". . . for those who help Jews, the punishment is harsh; imprisonment, perhaps"?

Teaching the Diary of Anne Frank   Scholastic Professional Books

The Secret Annexe

Anne first shared this room with Margot, then with Mr. Dussel.

The Frank and Van Daan families cooked and ate together here. This room, like Anne's room, was furnished after the war for the photographs. The rooms now stand empty.

The bookcase was added after July 6, 1942, when the Frank family moved into their hiding place. The stairs were concealed because of security concerns.

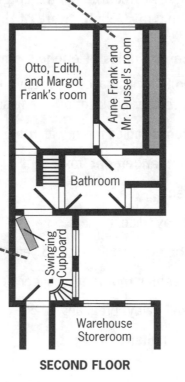

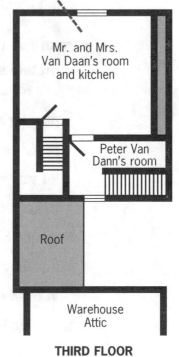

Otto, Edith, and Margot Frank's room

Anne Frank and Mr. Dussel's room

Bathroom

Swinging Cupboard

Warehouse Storeroom

SECOND FLOOR

Mr. and Mrs. Van Daan's room and kitchen

Peter Van Dann's room

Roof

Warehouse Attic

THIRD FLOOR

About Language at War

Do you know what *doublespeak* means? The word was coined by George Orwell, author of *1984*, to describe language that is used in a deceptive way. In *Politics and the English Language*, Orwell lists "swindles and perversions" of language. He says that "the great enemy of clear language is insincerity. When there is a gap between one's real and one's declared aims, one turns as it were instinctively to long words and exhausted idioms, like a [squid] squirting out ink."

Euphemisms like those in the Language at War listing are a common form of doublespeak. It's not hard to find examples today. Newspapers quoting politicians and government officials are filled with them. Just listen to sound bites on television and radio.

The National Council of Teachers of English issues "doublespeak awards" from time to time. And many newspapers print a list of the most outrageous examples among the award winners. Doublespeak corrupts communication among people just as forgeries corrupt the exchange of money. Our best protection against language abuses is uncovering examples and making people aware of them.

Here are some examples of euphemisms:

protein spill an insurance company's reference to people killed in a roller coaster accident at an amusement park

powder room ladies room, bathroom

revenue enhancement taxes

let go fired

passed away died

senior citizens people over 65 years old

having a senior moment younger people having a brief memory lapse

in the family way pregnant

vertically challenged short

Teaching the Diary of Anne Frank Scholastic Professional Books

Language at War

The decision makers among the Nazis made every effort to keep their plans for the destruction of Europe's Jews a secret. The Nazis' use of euphemisms (inoffensive language used to mask offensive meanings) like the examples below was part of a careful effort to disguise the truth.

WHAT THE NAZIS SAID (EUPHEMISM)	WHAT THEY MEANT
Jewish residential quarters	**ghettos**
resettlement resettlement action evacuation emigration deportation labor in the east	**deportation to killing centers**
the east labor camp concentration camp transit camp (Sobibor)	**killing centers**
special installations special buildings bathhouses showers	**gas chambers/ crematoria**
final solution special treatment liquidation special actions cleansing operation	**killing**
an area free of Jews	**all Jews have been killed**

Talk It Over

1. Why did the Nazis use terms like the ones listed above?

2. Why didn't people question what these expressions meant?

3. Are there ever situations when using euphemisms is acceptable?

4. Anne reports that Margot received a call-up for resettlement for labor in the east (July 8, 1942). Did Margot and her family understand what that meant? How can you tell?

Teaching the Diary of Anne Frank   Scholastic Professional Books

A "Complete Solution"

1943: Field Marshal Hermann Goering (left) and Dr. Joseph Goebbels giving the Nazi salute

In 1941, Hermann Goering, the second-highest ranking Nazi after Adolf Hitler, sent the following order to Reinhard Heydrich, head of the Security Police. By the time this official permission arrived, Heydrich was already receiving reports from his mobile killing units called *einsatzgruppen*, advancing with the German army in Russia, that they were gassing and shooting Jews.

Berlin, 31. July 1941

The Reich Marshal of the Greater German Reich
Commissioner for the Four Year Plan
Chairman of the Ministerial Council for National Defense

To: The Chief of the Security Police and the Security Service;
SS-Gruppenfuehrer HEYDRICH

Complementing the task that was assigned to you on 24 January 1939, which dealt with arriving at, through furtherance of **emigration** and **evacuation**, a **solution of the Jewish problem**, as advantageous as possible, I hereby charge you with making **all necessary preparations** in regard to organizational and financial matters for bringing about **a complete solution of the Jewish question** in the German sphere of influence in Europe.
Whenever other governmental agencies are involved, these are to cooperate with you.
I charge you furthermore to send me, before long, an overall plan concerning the organizational, factual and material **measures necessary** for the **accomplishment of the desired solution of the Jewish question.**

signed: Goering

- -

CERTIFICATE OF TRANSLATION OF DOCUMENT NO. 710-PS

15 October 1945

I, FRED NIEBERGALL, 2nd Lt Inf, 0-1335567, hereby certify that I am thoroughly conversant with the English and German languages; and that the above is a true and correct translation of Document 710-PS.

/s/ Fred Niebergall
FRED NIEBERGALL
2nd Lt Inf, 0-133556

Source: National Archives [EMPHASIS ADDED]

Talk It Over

1. Explain the euphemisms highlighted in this document.

2. What did the euphemisms really mean? Why were these expressions used in correspondence between two high-ranking Nazis? Why didn't they just write what they really meant?

3. How can you tell this document was used as evidence in war crimes? What is the reason for the translation information later attached to it?

Teaching the Diary of Anne Frank   Scholastic Professional Books

Tuesday, November 10, 1942–Sunday, June 13, 1943

❖ Summary

Entries cover the period from Mr. Dussel's arrival to Anne's fourteenth birthday. Many entries focus on her relationship with adults, especially her parents, and her feelings about herself.

❖ Notes on the Diary

Share this information with students.

November 28, 1942: Electricity rationing
Beginning in 1941, the use of electricity and gas in the Netherlands was restricted by law. The penalty for using too much of either was loss of service.

December 7, 1942: Chanukah and St. Nicholas Day
Chanukah is the eight-day Jewish festival of lights, a celebration of the rededication of the Temple in Jerusalem in 165 B.C. The date of Chanukah is determined by the Jewish calendar. St. Nicholas Day, December 6, is the traditional day for Christmas gift giving in the Netherlands and other northern European countries.

January 13, March 10, 1943: Bombing raids, A.A. guns
Allied bombers flew over the Netherlands on their way from England to targets in Germany. The Allies also bombed docks, factories, and transportation centers in the Netherlands itself. The Germans defended vulnerable targets in the Netherlands with A.A. (antiaircraft) guns.

February 27, 1943: Bishop's letter
On Sunday, February 21, 1943, a message was read in all Catholic churches (and many Protestant churches as well) protesting the rounding up of young people and the persecution of the Jews.

March 27, 1943: Rauter
Anne refers to Hanns Rauter, head of the German SS (the Nazi militia) and police in the Netherlands.

Hanns Rauter (right)

❖ Guided Reading Questions

As they read the assigned entries, have students consider these questions and note their responses in their journals.

1. What restrictions did Anne have to put up with in hiding? What did she find most difficult about being in hiding?

2. How did Mr. Dussel adjust to life in the Secret Annexe? How did the war affect the lives of people in the Secret Annexe?

❖ Discussion Questions

- Anne writes on December 13, 1942, that she saw two Jews in the street below. How did she know they were Jews?

- What does Anne say about the fate of the Jews and her own situation on November 19 and 20, 1942 and January 13, 1943? Do her feelings change?

- On March 27, 1943, Anne quotes Hanns Rauter, a high-ranking Nazi, saying: "'All Jews must be out of the German-occupied countries before July 1. Between April 1 and May 1 the province of Utrecht [in the Netherlands] must be cleaned out. Between May 1 and June 1 the provinces of North and South Holland.'" What euphemism does Rauter use? Does Anne see through the veil of language to the truth underneath? How can you tell?

- What are your impressions of Anne at this point in the diary?

- Explain Anne's statement that none of those in hiding had ever celebrated St. Nicholas Day before (December 7, 1942).

❖ Response Journal Ideas

- Anne quotes her mother as saying "love cannot be forced" (April 2, 1943). What do you think this means?

- How would Anne's mother or Mr. Dussel describe Anne?

- When you look at the lists of numbers of Jews killed in the Holocaust they really are "Nameless Numbers." Compare Anne's diary to the cold lists of numbers (page 64). Which document (considering the diary as a document) has more impact on you? Why? What are some other ways to put names and faces to the horrors of the Holocaust?

❖ Projects

■ How did Anne's life change during her first year in hiding? The diary entries from June 12, 1942 through June 13, 1943 will help students answer this question. Ask students to consider food, living arrangements, school, socializing, health, and relationships with others.

■ Start with the proposition that the Holocaust was not inevitable, that even after the Wannsee Conference, the stepped-up annihilation stage of the Holocaust could have been avoided. Can students think of reasons the people gathered at the Wannsee Conference believed that this ambitious plan would work? The plan required the cooperation of the entire German bureaucracy. Why were the planners sure that everyone would cooperate? Ask students to speculate about the answers. Some students may want to research the reactions of European governments to the Nazis' treatment of Jews and learn how attitudes changed over the years of the Holocaust.

❖ Resource Pages

Excerpt from the Wannsee Protocol, 1/20/42

The plan to kill all of Europe's Jews began rather quietly, secretly. On January 20, 1942, at Wannsee 56-58, a private villa on the outskirts of Berlin, 15 high-ranking Nazis met. The topic of the Wannsee Conference was "The Final Solution of the Jewish Problem (for all European Jewry)." This innocuous wording was a code for the destruction of the Jews. The conferees met to coordinate their efforts in different parts of Nazi-controlled Europe, to make them more efficient. The protocol, or action plan, that resulted from the conference included this country-by-country list of Jews slated for destruction (page 63).

Translation of Document No. NG-2536 and The Nameless Numbers Speak (pages 63–64) show the horrifying results of bureaucratic decisions reached at the Wannsee Conference.

This document was used as evidence at the war crimes trials at Nuremberg after World War II.

Talk It Over

1. Look at the Language at War page to help you discuss the euphemisms in the Wannsee Protocol, such as "evacuation to the east" and "final solution." Why did the Nazis find euphemisms necessary? What might have happened if they had said exactly what they meant?

2. Check the time line: When were the extermination camps built?

3. Explain the significance of the fact that the list in the Wannsee Protocol includes all the European countries, even those not occupied by the Germans.

4. Use a map of the period to identify which countries listed were not under German domination in January 1942. Then identify those that were never under German control.

5. Why were there no Jews in Estonia? In German, the notation next to Estonia says *judenfrei* (YOU-den-fry—"free of Jews"). Is that a euphemism?

6. How did the Nazi leaders know how many Jews there were in countries under their control? In countries not under their control?

7. Why are there more Jews listed in unoccupied France than in occupied France?

Teaching the Diary of Anne Frank   Scholastic Professional Books

TRANSLATION OF DOCUMENT NO. NG-2536

III. Another possible solution of the problem has now taken the place of emigration, i.e. the evacuation of the Jews to the East, provided the Fuehrer agrees to this plan....

Approx[imately] 11,000,000 Jews will be involved in this final solution of the European problem, they are to be distributed as follows among the countries:

Country	Number
A Germany proper	131,800
Austria	43,700
Eastern territories [Poland]	420,000
General Government [Poland]	2,284,000
Bialystok	400,000
Protectorate, Bohemia & Moravia	74,200
Estonia	no Jews
Latvia	3,500
Lithuania	34,000
Belgium	43,000
Denmark	5,600
France/Occupied France	165,000
Unoccupied France	700,000
Greece	69,600
Netherlands	160,800
Norway	1,300
B Bulgaria	48,000
England	330,000
Finland	2,300
Ireland	4,000
Italy incl. Sardinia	58,000
Albania	200
Croatia	40,000
Portugal	43,000
Romania, incl. Bessarabia	342,000
Sweden	8,000
Switzerland	18,000
Serbia	10,000
Slovakia	88,000
Spain	6,000
Turkey (European Turkey)	55,500
Hungary	742,800
USSR	5,000,000
Ukraine	2,994,684
White Russia with exception of Bialystok	446,484

Source: National Archives

*Total: over 11,000,000

* Note: These numbers actually total more than 14,000,000. In fact, a more accurate accounting of Jews in Europe before World War II is 9,000,000, of whom almost 6,000,000, or 67 percent, were killed by the Nazis. See Resource Page, The Nameless Numbers Speak.

Teaching the Diary of Anne Frank   Scholastic Professional Books

The Nameless Numbers Speak

Estimated Number of Jews Killed in the Final Solution

Country	Pre–Final Solution Population	Estimated Jewish Population Annihilated	
		Number	Percent
Poland	3,300,000	3,000,000	90
Baltic Countries	250,000	228,000	90
Germany/Austria	240,000	210,000	90
Protectorate	90,000	80,000	89
Slovakia	90,000	75,000	83
Greece	70,000	54,000	77
Netherlands	140,000	105,000	75
Hungary	650,000	450,000	70
SSR White Russia	375,000	245,000	65
SSR Ukraine*	1,500,000	900,000	60
Belgium	65,000	40,000	60
Yugoslavia	43,000	26,000	60
Romania	600,000	300,000	50
Norway	1,800	900	50
France	350,000	90,000	26
Bulgaria	64,000	14,000	22
Italy	40,000	8,000	20
Luxembourg	5,000	1,000	20
Russia*	975,000	107,000	11
Denmark	7,000	—	—
Finland	2,000	—	—
Total:	**8,857,800**	**5,933,900**	**67**

* The Germans did not occupy all the territory of this republic.

From *The War Against the Jews* by Lucy S. Dawidowicz. Copyright © 1962 by Lucy S. Dawidowicz. Reprinted by permission of Henry Holt & Co., Inc.

Teaching the Diary of Anne Frank   Scholastic Professional Books

Hitler Orders Silence

This secret document was used in the prosecution of Nazi war criminals during the Nuremberg trials. It shows the extent of Hitler's control over speech and his fanatical concern that no one in his government reveal the true fate of Europe's Jews. Aside from Hitler's speeches and writings, war crimes investigators found few documents tying Hitler directly to the day-to-day operations of the Holocaust. This is a translation of one of them.

National-Socialist German Workers' Party
Party Secretariat

Head of the Party Secretariat   Fuhrer headquarters,
July 11, 1943

Circular No. 33/43 g.

Re: Treatment of the Jewish Question

On instructions from the Fuhrer I make known the following: Where the Jewish Question is brought up in public, there may be no discussion of a future overall solution.

It may however be mentioned that the Jews are taken in groups for appropriate labor purposes.

                 signed M. Bormann

Distribution: Reichsleiter
                 Gauleiter [managers of political districts]
                 Group leaders

File reference: Treatment/Jews
[National Archives; NO2710]

Talk It Over

1. What are the euphemisms in this memo?

2. Why do you think Hitler distanced himself, on paper, from the actual killing of the Jews?

Reading 4

(pages 83–127)

Tuesday, June 15, 1943–Wednesday, December 29, 1943

❖ Summary

These entries include reflective and descriptive "typical day" reports, Anne's experiments with writing, and powerful descriptions of her dreams and fears about the war.

❖ Note on the Diary

Share this information with students.

Page 92: Bombing of Amsterdam

Two critical targets for Allied bombers are mentioned here: the Fokker aircraft plant and Schiphol, Amsterdam airport.

❖ Guided Reading Questions

As they read the assigned diary entries, have students consider these questions and note their responses in their journals.

1. In what ways do Anne's descriptions of life in the Secret Annexe during this period differ from earlier entries?

2. What frustrations with her life in hiding does Anne describe during this period?

❖ Discussion Questions

- Anne reports on her attempts at negotiation with Mr. Dussel over the use of the table in their shared room (July 13, 1943). Does it seem to you that she is in the right? How would Mr. Dussel describe the argument?

- Why do you think Anne prepares an "escape bag" (July 26, 1943) when she admits the streets are "just as dangerous as an air raid"?

- Discuss Anne's diary entry for December 24, 1943. Do you believe Anne when she says she is not jealous of Corry Koophuis?

- How do Anne's dreams about her friend Lies (November 27, 1943) and her grandmother (December 29, 1943) affect her feelings about her life?

❖ Response Journal Ideas

■ What kind of person do you think Anne is? Anne describes herself as a "coward" (November 8, 1943) and "selfish" (December 29, 1943). What other words does she use to describe herself? What words would you use, based on what you have read so far?

■ How did you react to Anne's dreams or to Anne's statement at the end of the entry for November 8, 1943 that the Secret Annexe is "a little piece of blue heaven, surrounded by heavy black rain clouds"?

■ Describe a dream that you've had that held a lot of meaning for you.

■ Comment on the idea that Anne's diary keeping was an act of spiritual resistance.

❖ Project

"A Little Piece of Blue Heaven, Surrounded by Heavy Black Rain Clouds"
Write a poem or create a drawing that illustrates the meaning of—and your reactions to—Anne's description of her life in the Secret Annexe. What strikes you most forcibly? Her fears of being trapped during an air raid? Her fear of discovery? The quarrels among the people hiding? The lack of food? The relative safety of the Secret Annexe?

❖ Resource Pages

Call for Diaries in the Warsaw Ghetto (page 69)

I Want My Little Daughter to Be Remembered (page 70)

The Butterfly (page 71)

Life—and Death— in the Ghettos

After 1939, when the Germans invaded Poland, the concentration stage of the Holocaust went into high gear. Jews living in the countryside were directed to gather in cities, and non-Jews in certain sections of the cities were forced to move. The cleared areas where the Jews were forced to settle were the ghettos. The Nazis walled these sections off, imprisoning the Jews inside.

Unlike ghettos in medieval times, when Jews were confined only at night and allowed out to work during the day, the Nazi ghettos let no one in or out. Outside the walls, people went on about their business. Inside the ghettos, conditions were horrendous. Often, many families were crowded together in one apartment. Food was scarce; there was limited medical care. Over all hung a feeling of dread. The Warsaw ghetto was the largest, covering an area of about one square mile. In that area lived 350,000 Jews.

Slave labor was another aspect of ghetto life. All Jewish men and women from age 14 to 65 were required to work for free. Many industrial giants like I. G. Farben and Krupp contracted with the SS for free Jewish labor and built factories near the ghettos (and later near concentration camps). Jews were expected to work long hours on very little food and under the harshest conditions. Many slave laborers died before they were deported to the killing centers. An exception were the slave laborers who worked for Oskar Schindler. (See The Story of Oskar Schindler, page 53.)

Spiritual resistance was an important part of ghetto life. Despite cold, hunger, and disease, the Jews in the ghetto organized secret schools, religious services, underground newspapers, and smuggling operations. Children were often used to sneak out of the ghetto for supplies. If caught, they were shot by the Germans. Emanuel Ringenblum, a historian confined in the ghetto, organized an effort to keep detailed records of life there. In the Warsaw ghetto, and other places, these records were concealed and buried at great risk to the people who hid them.

Uprising in the Warsaw Ghetto, 1943

They did not go quietly to the gas chambers. In April and May 1943, residents of the Warsaw ghetto began a fiercely fought armed challenge to the Nazis.

More than 300,000 people from the ghetto were deported in 1942. The revolt was sparked by the Germans' decision to "liquidate" the ghetto by deporting the Jews who remained.

For 28 days the Jews held off their heavily armed oppressors with weapons provided by the Polish resistance and smuggled in from outside the ghetto walls. On the first day of the revolt, ghetto fighters posted on the roofs of buildings drove out a German force of more than 2,000 SS and police units.

The organized ghetto fighters, from 700 to 800 men and women, were protecting thousands of Jews hidden underground in reinforced cellars. Some of the cellars were connected to city sewers that could be used as escape routes. The well-coordinated uprising took the Nazis by surprise. As the confrontations continued, they retaliated by burning down the ghetto, depriving the fighters of their rooftop positions. One historian wrote of the Warsaw ghetto uprising this way:

> Tens of thousands of ghetto residents took part in the revolt and identified with it. They transformed the ghetto into an indomitable fortress from which they had to be extracted one by one, requiring thousands of German troops—who suffered losses. The struggle went on for weeks, and this uprising of the last Jews in Warsaw became the first mass revolt in Nazi-occupied Europe. Its message extended far beyond the walls of the ruined ghetto.

Source of quotation: *The Holocaust* by Leni Yahil, Oxford University Press, New York, 1990

Under the watchful eyes of Nazis, Jewish people are driven from a ghetto.

Call for Diaries in the Warsaw Ghetto

In the Warsaw ghetto, members of a group code named Oneg Shabbat (In Praise of the Sabbath) kept records of everything that was happening to Jews in Poland. They encouraged ordinary people, not just historians and writers, to document life in the ghetto. The materials Oneg Shabbat collected were buried in metal containers inside the ghetto. Some were recovered after the war. One Oneg Shabbat worker wrote:

> . . . I regard it as a sacred task . . . for everyone, whether or not he has the ability, to write down everything he has witnessed or has heard from those who have witnessed—the atrocities which the barbarians committed in every Jewish town. When the time will come—and indeed it will surely come—let the world read and know what the murderers perpetrated. This will be the richest material for the mourner when he writes the elegy for the present time. This will be the most powerful subject matter for the avenger. . . . We are obligated to assist them, to help them, even if we must pay with our own lives, which today are very cheap.

Talk It Over

1. Think about the concept of spiritual resistance that was introduced earlier. What did living in a ghetto mean for Jewish people? What possibilities for resistance were available?

2. According to the author, which residents of the ghetto should keep a diary? Why does the author believe firsthand accounts of what happened were important?

3. Who are the "barbarians" in the first sentence? The "mourner" in the third sentence? The "avenger" in the fourth sentence?

4. What does the writer mean when he says "our own lives . . . are very cheap"?

I Want My Little Daughter to Be Remembered (Israel Lichtenstein's Last Testament)

Israel Lichtenstein, a teacher, was one of the secret historians of Oneg Shabbat in the Warsaw ghetto. He wrote an account of days in July 1942, when thousands of Jews were forcibly removed from the Warsaw ghetto and sent to Treblinka, a death camp. Knowing that he and his family would be killed, Israel Lichtenstein added this testament to his other writings.

With zeal and zest I threw myself into the work to help assemble archive materials. I was entrusted to be the custodian, I hid the material. Besides me, no one knew. I confided only in my friend Hersh Wasser, my superior.

It is well hidden. Please God that it be preserved. That will be the finest and best that we achieved in the present gruesome time.

I know that we will not endure. To survive and remain alive [after] such horrible murders and massacres is impossible. Therefore I write this testament of mine. . . .

I want my wife to be remembered. Gele Seckstein, artist, dozens of works, talented, didn't manage to exhibit, did not show in public.

During the three years of war worked among children as educator, teacher, made stage sets, costumes for the children's production, received awards. Now together with me, we are preparing to receive death.

Margalit, 20 months old today. Has mastered Yiddish perfectly, speaks a pure Yiddish. At 9 months began to speak Yiddish clearly. In intelligence she is on a par with 3- or 4-year-old children. I don't want to brag about her. Witnesses to this, who tell me about it, are the teaching staff of the school at Nowolipki 68.

I am not sorry about my life and that of my wife. But I am sorry for the gifted little girl. She deserves to be remembered also.

May we be the redeemers for all the rest of the Jews in the whole world. I believe in the survival of our people. Jews will not be annihilated. We, the Jews of Poland, Czechoslovakia, Lithuania, Latvia, are the scapegoat for all Israel in all the other lands.

—*July 31, 1942 The eleventh day of the so-called "resettlement action." In reality, an annihilation action.*

Talk It Over

1. Why did Israel Lichtenstein write this testament and what did he do with it when he was finished?

2. What service did Lichtenstein perform in the ghetto?

3. Why was he convinced that he and his wife and child would die?

4. What do the choppy sentences in paragraphs 5 and 6 tell you about the author's frame of mind when he wrote this document?

5. Why was it important that ghetto prisoners kept a record of what happened? In what ways do oral history projects, such as Steven Spielberg's Shoah project (and other survivors' oral histories), carry on Oneg Shabbat's mission?

6. In what ways was this last testament an act of spiritual resistance?

7. How does the fact that you're reading what Israel Lichtenstein wrote affirm his spiritual resistance?

"Israel Lichtenstein's Last Testament" from *Wasser Collection, YIVO Archives* (YIVO Institute for Jewish Research, New York). Appears in *A Holocaust Reader* edited by Lucy Dawidowicz. Selection translated by Lucy Dawidowicz. By permission of Behrman House, Inc.

Teaching the Diary of Anne Frank   Scholastic Professional Books

The Butterfly

The author of this poem, Pavel Friedman, was 21 when he was deported to the Theresienstadt ghetto in 1942. Theresienstadt was a showcase "resettlement program," designed to fool observers like the International Red Cross about its real purpose. Because of that, some cultural activities were allowed.

Theresienstadt was really a transit camp, from which 88,162 people (out of 141,162) were transported to death camps. Of 12,000 children transported to Theresienstadt and housed there apart from their parents, only about 2,000 survived. By the end of the war in May 1945, another 33,456 people had died in the camp.

Pavel Friedman was deported from Theresienstadt to Auschwitz. There he was killed on September 29, 1944.

Talk It Over

1. What are the symbols in "The Butterfly"? What does each represent? Are the symbols related?

2. After you read the two other selections, compare them to Pavel Friedman's poem. Although the authors were in different ghettos, does "The Butterfly" in any way answer "the call for diaries" issued in the Warsaw ghetto? In what ways do the creation and preservation of these three documents—"The Butterfly," Call for Diaries, and I Want My Little Daughter to Be Remembered—represent acts of spiritual resistance to the Holocaust?

The Butterfly

The last, the very last,
So richly, brightly, dazzlingly yellow . . .
Perhaps if the sun's tears would sing
against a white stone . . .

Such, such a yellow
Is carried lightly 'way up high.
It went away I'm sure because it wished to
kiss the world good-bye.

For seven weeks I've lived in here
Penned up inside this ghetto
But I have found my people here.
The dandelions call to me
And the white chestnut candles* in the court.
Only I never saw another butterfly.

That butterfly was the last one.
Butterflies don't live in here,
In the ghetto.

—*Pavel Friedman*
June 4, 1942

* "White chestnut candles" refers to the white buds of the chestnut tree, which look like candles.

Teaching the Diary of Anne Frank Scholastic Professional Books

Reading 5

Sunday, January 2, 1944–Tuesday, March 28, 1944

❖ Summary

Entries focus on Anne's feelings about Peter as their relationship develops.

❖ Notes on the Diary

Share this information with students.

February 3, 1944: "Invasion fever in the country is mounting daily."
By 1943, many people felt it was just a matter of time before Hitler and the Germans were defeated. A key element in that defeat was widely recognized to be an invasion of Europe by the Allied forces. Throughout the spring of 1944, people speculated about when and where the Allies would mount their invasion. Operation Overlord, the invasion of Normandy in early June, was successfully planned and launched without the Germans' knowledge.

March 14, 1944: Coupons and ration cards
During wartime when food was scarce, authorities tried to ensure fair distribution of meat, sugar, butter, coffee, and other staples by rationing them. Citizens had to register to receive ration cards and allotments of coupons, enough to last one or two months. They had to present these documents along with payment in order to receive food. Because they were in hiding, people in the Secret Annexe relied on people in the Dutch Resistance to provide them with forged coupons.

Peter Van Daan

❖ Guided Reading Questions

As they read the assigned diary entries, have students consider these questions and note their responses in their journals.

1. How did Anne's feelings about Peter affect her relationships with the others in the Secret Annexe?

2. How did their surroundings affect Anne and Peter's relationship?

3. How did Anne describe the natural world in this selection?

❖ Discussion Questions

■ Compare Anne's thoughts on living in hiding on January 28, 1944, with earlier entries about life in hiding.

- On March 17, 1944, Anne writes about wanting to be independent. What does the word *independence* mean to you? How has its meaning changed for you as you've grown up?

❖ Response Journal Ideas

- On January 2, 1944, Anne writes about how valuable the diary is to her. Write a letter to Anne telling her the ways her diary is valuable to you.

- Anne writes about seeing herself through someone else's eyes (January 12, 1944). Describe yourself through someone else's eyes—a parent's view, for example, or that of a close friend or a sibling.

- On February 12 and 13, 1944, Anne writes of her longing to be alone. Write about a time when you wanted to say, "Leave me in peace, leave me alone," as Anne does. Describe a place where you can go to be alone. Reflect on Anne's last sentence of the entry for that date: "Who knows, the day may come when I'm left alone more than I would wish!"

- On March 20 and 22, 1944, Anne copies into her diary the letters she and Margot exchanged in the Secret Annexe. Write your own letter to Anne and share it with the class.

- Although they were Jewish girls of almost the same age in Nazi-occupied countries, Anne Frank and Jenny Misuchin (see page 78) had very different experiences. Reflect on the differences between their situations.

❖ Project

The Way It Was How do personal reminiscences help historians and authors? Create a class time capsule. Include statements and small artifacts that will give future historians a sense of what it's like to be a young person right now. As a class, make these decisions: When do you want the time capsule opened—2010? 2025? 2050? Should each person write his or her own thoughts and impressions, or do you want to assign individuals to write on specific topics, such as politics, the economy, world affairs, entertainment, recreation, or a typical day? Arrange with your school administration, local library, or local government to preserve your time capsule until the date you specify.

❖ Resource Pages

Homeless

In "Homeless," an anonymous author describes the deportation of 10,000 Jews from the Bedzin ghetto on August 12, 1942. The author and other able-bodied young people were selected for slave labor, while the rest went to their deaths at Auschwitz. The words were set to music and sung in the Bedzin ghetto and slave labor camps.

Talk It Over

1. What events is the author describing?

2. How does this poem measure up as an eyewitness account asked for in the Call for Diaries?

"Homeless" from *Pinkes Bendin*, ed. A. S. Stein, Tel Aviv, 1959. Appears in *A Holocaust Reader* edited by Lucy Dawidowicz. Selection translated by Lucy Dawidowicz. By permission of Behrman House, Inc.

Homeless

Without a home, without a roof—
We tramped the whole night through,
Not knowing whereto
Or what our end would be.

At the station we were jammed in a pack
And held in leash by the SS police;
How much longer will our pain last?
Hell-fire surely can't be worse!

Without a home, without a roof . . .

No bread, no water did we get
They kept us there a day, a night,
Children torn from their mothers' arms
And dragged off who knows where.

Without a home, without a roof . . .

They hound us, they harass us,
They torment and torture us,
This is how they draw our blood.
For without a home, without a roof . . .
To that staging area they drove us
And selected us like sheep;
Torn away from our parents
We the young were herded to the camps.

Without a home, without a roof,
We tramped the whole night through—
Not knowing whereto
Or what our end would be.

—*Anonymous*

Teaching the Diary of Anne Frank Scholastic Professional Books

A Dead Child Speaks

"Ein Totes Kind Spricht"

Nelly Sachs left Germany in 1940 and with the help of the novelist Selma Lagerlof spent the remainder of the war in Sweden. There she wrote many moving poems about the fate of European Jews at the hands of the Nazis. In 1966 she received the Nobel Prize for Literature. This poem is from her book of poems *O the Chimneys.*

Nelly Sachs

A Dead Child Speaks

My mother held me by the hand.
Then someone held the knife of parting:
So that it should not strike me,
My mother loosed her hand from mine.
But she lightly touched my thighs once more
And her hand was bleeding—

After that the knife of parting
Cut in two each bite I swallowed—
It rose before me with the sun at dawn
And began to sharpen itself in my eyes—
Wind and water ground in my ear
And every voice of comfort pierced my heart—

As I was led to death
I still felt in the last moment
The unsheathing of the great knife of parting.

—*Nelly Sachs*

Talk It Over

1. What do you think the poet means by the title?

2. What is the "knife of parting"?

3. What does the poet mean when she says: "After that the knife of parting/Cut in two each bite I swallowed— . . . And every voice of comfort pierced my heart"?

4. What are some ways this poem differs from "Homeless"?

Teaching the Diary of Anne Frank Scholastic Professional Books

Eyewitnesses at Auschwitz-Birkenau

Alfred Weczler and Rudolf Vrba

In the spring of 1944, two Slovakian prisoners, Alfred Weczler and Rudolf Vrba, escaped from the killing center at Auschwitz and revealed what was really happening there behind the screen of Nazi doublespeak. They were among a very small number of people who successfully escaped from a killing center. This was an extraordinary act of resistance, depriving the killing machine of two victims and making the elaborately protected secret of the final solution known to the world. Their firsthand account of what was happening to the Jews transported to Auschwitz confirmed what many outside the camps already suspected. But, compelling and detailed as this information was, no action was taken by the Allied powers to stop the killing.

This excerpt from their 40-page typed report describes the actual gassing of Jews at Birkenau, part of the immense Auschwitz camp. Men, women, and children from all over Europe, Jews and non-Jews, were brought to Auschwitz by the trainload. They first went through a selection process to determine who would live (for a while) and who would die immediately. Selections were based on physical appearance rather than age. Children who looked younger than 15 were automatically sent to be killed along with their mothers, as were the elderly or any who looked frail, no matter what their age. Those selected were told they were going through a disinfecting shower, after which they would be housed in the camp.

At the end of February 1943, a new modern crematorium and gassing plant were inaugurated at Birkenau. . . .

At present four crematoria are in operation at Birkenau, two large ones, I and II, and two smaller ones, III and IV. . . .

The gassing takes place as follows: the unfortunate victims [men, women, and children] are brought into the reception hall where they are told to undress. To complete the fiction that they are going to bathe, each person receives a towel and a small piece of soap issued by two men in white coats. Then they are crowded into the gas chamber in such numbers that there is, of course, only standing room. To compress this crowd into the narrow space, shots are often fired to induce those at the far end to huddle closer together. When everybody is inside, the heavy doors are closed. Then there is a short pause, presumably to allow the room temperature to rise to a certain level, after which SS men [killing center guards] with gas masks climb on the roof, open the traps, and shake down a preparation in powder form out of tin cans labeled "Zyklon—For use against vermin," manufactured by a Hamburg concern. It is presumed that this is a

Teaching the Diary of Anne Frank   Scholastic Professional Books

cyanide mixture of some sort which turns into gas at a certain temperature. After three minutes [other reports are as high as 30 minutes] everyone in the chamber is dead. No one is known to have survived this ordeal. . . . The chamber is then opened, aired, and the Sonderkommando [a group of prisoners assigned to the task of transporting the dead] carts the bodies on flat trucks to the furnace rooms where the burning takes place. . . . The total capacity of the four gassing and cremating plants at Birkenau amounts to about 6,000 daily. . . .

Cautious estimate of the number of Jews gassed in Birkenau between April 1942 and April 1944 . . . 1,765,000.

An old railway sign leads the way to Auschwitz, a death camp in Poland.

Talk It Over

1. How do you think the Allied powers received this information? Do you think anything was done as a result of this report? Why do you think this is true?

2. How does the objective style of the report add to its believability?

3. In what ways are the soap and towels and men in white coats similar to euphemisms like "resettlement" and "labor camp"?

Teaching the Diary of Anne Frank   Scholastic Professional Books

Report by Alfred Weczler and Rudolf Vrba to the United States War Refugee Board, November 1944, "German Extermination Camps—Auschwitz and Birkenau."

Jenny Misuchin— Jewish Resistance Fighter

Some Jews escaped from the ghettos and joined forces with partisans, which were small, organized groups, often with Soviet army contacts and weapons, who lived in the woods and mountains of Eastern Europe. Partisans disrupted communication and transportation lines, gathered intelligence, and harassed the German army and SS whenever they could. Jewish partisans either became part of non-Jewish groups or formed groups of their own. In both cases, the Jewish resisters fought two enemies: the Nazis and the anti-Semitic people they encountered— sometimes other partisans, sometimes farmers whom the partisans asked for food and shelter. While most partisans were men, many women like Jenny also joined the fight. Jenny survived the war. In 1987 she told her story to a reporter. The quotations are from his article about her.

"It was June, 1941, in Vidze, Lithuania, and a pretty 15-year-old girl with wavy shoulder-length brown hair and bright green eyes is looking forward to the end of school and summer vacation. . . . Jenny Misuchin lived in a lovely green town in a valley with white sidewalks and chestnut trees and flower gardens. Her parents, Azriel and Luba, were protective. . . only recently had she been allowed to wear the 'student heels' which many of her girlfriends were already wearing."

Jenny's peaceful world was shattered on June 22 when German storm troopers appeared in town. First Jenny's father was taken away and shot. Then Jenny, her mother and brother and sister, along with other Jews from Vidze, were deported to a larger town where Jenny was assigned to a job in a factory. It was there she first met members of the Jewish resistance, people dedicated to fighting the German soldiers. One of them gave her a hand grenade, which she carefully hid. But she did not join the resistance right away. She waited until it was almost too late. Just as she was about to be deported again with her mother, sister, and brother, she slipped away from the train station. She never saw them again. That time Jenny was caught and sent to work on a farm. She escaped from the farm disguised as a peasant girl. In the thick woods, she met a group of resistance fighters, or partisans, who agreed take her in. She still had her hand grenade.

In the woods, Jenny "learned to find her way by the stars and to cover her tracks in mud and in snow. . . . She suffered frostbite in winter and exhaustion in summer. . . . [She] remembered the words of her mother after the death of her father, 'We must pay back blood for blood.'

Teaching the Diary of Anne Frank   Scholastic Professional Books

"Jenny went on missions with the partisans, blowing up bridges, derailing troop trains, cutting communications wires, nursing wounded partisans, taking revenge on collaborators [people who cooperated with the German soldiers]." In time, Jenny won the respect of the other partisans. When she was wounded, they refused to abandon her, although her injury slowed them down.

In June 1944 Jenny's unit marched to meet the advancing Soviet army, who were fighting the Germans—and winning. "On the road [we] were met by another partisan brigade, and another. Soon there were about two thousand. . . . Everyone was singing. . . ."

Jenny went back to her hometown of Vidze and testified in a trial against the man who had taken her father away to be shot. She married another Jewish resistance fighter and, about three years after the war ended, they came to the United States and settled in New York, where they established a successful retail clothing business.

Jenny says: "For many years I couldn't talk about what had happened, as though I had committed a crime by staying alive. My family and close friends have helped me erase some of those guilt feelings. . . . I can still hate with all my heart those people who robbed me of so much. But I can't let those feelings consume me. Otherwise Hitler has won."

Talk It Over

1. Why do you think the rest of her family stayed behind when Jenny slipped away from the other Jews waiting on the railroad platform to be deported?

2. How did Jenny manage to travel openly? Was that an option for all Jews?

3. Even though Jenny escaped death, do you think that she, like the child in Nelly Sachs's poem, experienced "the great knife of parting"? If so, when and where?

4. What did Jenny's mother mean when she said, "We must pay back blood for blood"? What does the word *revenge* mean? How do you think a person seeking revenge for her family's deaths must feel? Angry? Sad? Scared? Murderous?

5. Explain what you think Jenny means by this statement: "I can still hate with all my heart those people who robbed me of so much. But I can't let those feelings consume me. Otherwise Hitler has won."

Adapted and excerpted from "Happy Ending: From Lithuania to Little Neck—The Incredible Saga of a WWII Jewish Resistance Fighter" by Ira Berkow from the *New York Sunday News Magazine*, May 17, 1981. Copyright © 1981 by Ira Berkow. Used by permission of the publisher.

Wednesday, March 29, 1944–Tuesday, August 1, 1944

❖ Summary

This section starts with Anne's report of a BBC broadcast in which a Dutch cabinet minister announced that personal diaries and letters would be valuable records after the war. Other entries focus on Anne's feelings about Peter and on world events, such as renewed anti-Semitism in Holland and the Allied invasion of France on June 6. The entry on August 1 is the last entry before the arrest and deportation of the Franks and their friends on August 4.

❖ Notes on the Diary

Share this information with students.

Page 193: The fate of Hungarian Jews

Up until March 1944, the Jews of Hungary, under a pro-German Hungarian government, were not sent to death camps as were others in Europe. That changed when the Germans, impatient with what they saw as the Hungarian government's leanings toward neutrality, occupied Hungary. Immediately, the Germans began deporting Hungarian Jews to Auschwitz. By July 1944, 437,000 Jews had been deported. Ultimately, 70 percent of Hungarian Jews, more than 450,000 people, were deported or killed between March 1944 and April 1945. (Anne's figure of 1,000,000 was incorrect.)

Allied soldiers march into occupied countries on D-Day.

Page 244: D-Day, June 6, 1944

On June 6, 1944, combined Allied forces—British, American, and Canadian—under General Eisenhower attacked the Germans along the well-defended Normandy coast of France by land, sea, and air. This was Operation Overlord, the long-anticipated invasion of Europe that, with the corresponding attacks on Germany by Soviet forces in the east, finally led to Germany's surrender in May 1945.

Page 264: Attempt on Hitler's life

On July 20, 1944, an attempt on Hitler's life failed; Hitler was only shaken by the bomb designed to kill him. The plot was devised by a group of Germans opposed to Hitler—aristocrats, senior officers, and diplomats. The man who planted the bomb was Count von Stauffenberg, a wounded officer who was motivated to kill Hitler because of the atrocities he had observed when serving in the army in Eastern Europe. Because he held a trusted position, von Stauffenberg was able to get close enough to Hitler to place a briefcase containing a bomb under the table where Hitler sat. He and all the other conspirators were caught and executed.

❖ Guided Reading Questions

As they read the assigned diary entries, have students consider these questions and note their responses in their journals.

1. How do Anne's feelings about Peter seem to change during this period?

2. How do Anne's feelings about the war change during this section of the diary?

3. How do hopes for the Allied invasion and the invasion itself affect the residents of the Secret Annexe?

❖ Discussion Questions

- On March 29, Anne reports hearing on the BBC that the Dutch government in exile is interested in collecting personal diaries and letters after the war. Why would a personal diary, like Anne's, be considered an important historical record?

- Anne writes on March 29, "It would seem quite funny ten years after the war if we Jews were to tell how we lived and what we ate and talked about here." What might Anne mean by "funny"? What other words might she have used?

- On May 26, 1944, Anne says, "Let the end come, even if it is hard." How and why did her mood change with the June 6 entry?

- Trace Anne's relationship with Peter through these entries in 1944: February 13; March 19; April 14, 16, and 28; and July 15. How do her feelings for him change?

- When Anne received her diary on June 12, 1942, she wrote, "I hope I shall be able to confide in you completely, as I have never been able to do in anyone before, and I hope you will be a great support and comfort to me." After reading the entire diary, give examples of times when Anne seemed able to confide in it "completely" and of times when the diary was a "support and comfort" to her.

❖ Response Journal Ideas

- On April 4 and on May 3, 8, and 11, 1944, Anne writes about herself and her hopes and dreams for after the war. Write about your dreams for the future. Or address a journal entry to Anne, telling her about her success as a writer.

- On July 15, 1944, Anne writes about how it is harder for young people to be in hiding than for the adults. Comment on her reasons for making this statement. Why do you agree or disagree with what she says?

- Describe the feelings Anne expresses in her final diary entry on August 1, 1944. Explain what you think she meant by feeling that there were two Annes.

- Contrast Anne's often quoted statement on July 15, 1944 (page 263), "In spite of everything I still believe that people are really good at heart," with this statement from May 3, 1944: "There's in people simply an urge to destroy, an urge to kill, to murder and rage."

BACKGROUND

Who Was Raoul Wallenberg?

In 1944, Raoul Wallenberg, a 32-year-old Swedish businessman-diplomat, was sent to Hungary with a special mission. As the citizen of a neutral country, Wallenberg was authorized to issue passports and safe conduct passes to rescue Hungarian Jews from their German-occupied nation.

These documents spelled the difference between life and death. With Swedish papers, Jews could avoid deportation to Nazi death camps. Jewish and refugee organizations in the United States and Sweden helped in this mission. Once in Budapest, Wallenberg handed out Swedish passports and safe conduct passes to Hungarian Jews who flocked to the Swedish embassy. Wallenberg used his position to gain access to Nazi authorities and to bribe and intimidate them in his efforts to protect Jews. It is estimated that by his efforts Wallenberg saved tens of thousands Hungarian Jews.

At Wallenberg's urging, representatives of other neutral countries coordinated efforts to protect thousands of Jews. When he was target-ed for assassination by the Arrow Cross, a pro-Nazi organization, Wallenberg continued his rescue efforts from underground.

In January 1945, when the Soviet Army entered Budapest, Wallenberg went to meet with the commander of Soviet troops. He was never heard from again. Efforts to locate him were fruitless, but for years it was rumored that he was still alive. The Soviet government finally admitted that Wallenberg had been arrested. The Soviets, ever paranoid, may have thought Wallenberg was a spy. In 1991, a Soviet historian discovered that Wallenberg had been shot by the Soviet authorities at Lubianka prison in 1947.

For his heroic struggle to save the Jews of Hungary, Raoul Wallenberg was granted honorary citizenship in the United States. Winston Churchill is the only other foreigner to receive that honor.

- If the shoes at Auschwitz shown in the photograph (on page 86) could have spoken, what might they have said to their new owners?

❖ Project

Display some items that represent travel—a suitcase, a backpack, a passport, an airline boarding pass, a railroad timetable. Have students respond to these objects aloud or in writing: What do they have in common? What does it feel like to go on a trip? A vacation? To move to another place? Explain the purpose of a passport and visa (permission to exit and or enter a country). Then ask, "What did these things mean to Jews in Europe during the Holocaust? What, specifically, would they have meant to Anne Frank and her family?" Leave the display of travel items set up in the classroom and encourage students to create poems and drawings to show what these items might have meant to the Jews of Europe in the 1940s.

You might ask students to imagine what it was like to be a Jewish person who fled Nazi Germany for safety when flight was still possible. What things might such a person have taken in one or two small suitcases? (Some people took photo albums, small silver items, mementos, and books, for example.) What would students take if they sensed they might never be able to return home?

❖ Resource Pages

All They Had Left (page 84)

Inventory (page 85)

A Cartload of Shoes (page 86)

All They Had Left

Jews transported to the killing centers of Auschwitz-Birkenau, Treblinka, Chelmno, Sobibor, Madjanek, and Belzec were told to bring their valuables and other belongings with them in clearly marked suitcases, boxes, and bags. This made people think they were being "resettled" in labor camps or "evacuated farther east." The myth continued on the railway platforms at the killing centers, where they arrived hungry, thirsty, cold, and sick after standing in cattle cars, sometimes going for days without food, water, or sanitation. (The killing centers were built on railway lines to make it easier to bring victims to their death.)

On the platform, luggage was immediately taken away. The dazed passengers were told it would be returned to them. Instead it was opened and emptied. Every personal possession, from eyeglasses to photographs to women's hair, was confiscated by the camp authorities, sorted by prisoners, and shipped back to Germany for sale or distribution. Women's hair was used in equipment for German U-boat [submarine] crewmen.

People were also sorted—the able-bodied were separated from those destined to be killed immediately. The latter were hurried along by guards with whips and dogs, still being told that they were to receive disinfecting showers. At Auschwitz, upbeat music was played through loudspeakers to further fool the new arrivals. In an anteroom, people stripped, their belongings were confiscated, and they were herded into gas chambers. Those selected to be slave laborers were also stripped and issued rags or prisoners' uniforms.

One of the men assigned to sort through victims' belongings was Rudolf Vrba, who later escaped to tell the truth about Auschwitz. After the war he wrote:

> Slowly the bags and the clothes and the food and the sad, smiling photographs became people to me; the prams became babies and the heaps of carefully segregated little shoes became children, like my cousin, Lici, in Topolcany.

Source of quotation: Rudolf Vrba. *I Cannot Forgive*, Sidgwick & Jackson Ltd., Publishers (and Anthony Gibbs and Philips co-publishers).

Talk It Over

1. Who was Rudolf Vrba, the man quoted here?

2. What was the purpose of the Inventory on page 85? How do you think the person who counted the items was affected by what he or she was doing?

3. Jews and other victims being deported were given precise instructions about what they could bring with them—how many sets of underwear, for example—and how to mark their luggage. The instructions also stated: "Everything must be in good condition." Why was that instruction included? Do you think people being deported were suspicious of these instructions? If they did suspect something, what could they do?

4. What items in the Inventory on page 85 are you surprised to see there? Why?

5. Many of the clothes taken from Jews and other victims in the killing centers were given to Germans who had lost their belongings in Allied bombing raids. Do you think the recipients of these things asked about where they came from? If so, what might they have been told?

6. Why do you think the Inventory on page 85 is marked "Top Secret"? What do you think this document revealed to people who were investigating the Nazis' "crimes against humanity" for the Nuremberg trials?

Teaching the Diary of Anne Frank   Scholastic Professional Books

Inventory

Excerpts from the translation of Document NO-1257 used as evidence in a
war crimes trial conducted by the United States Military Tribunal at Nuremberg.

TOP SECRET   **6 February 1943**

List of Reusable Textiles from the Lublin (Majdanek) and Auschwitz concentration
camps requested by the SS Central Office for Economy and Administration (WVHA):

1. Reich Ministry of Economics

Men's used clothing without underwear	97,000 sets	
Women's used clothing without underwear	76,000 sets	
Women's silk lingerie	89,000 sets	
SUBTOTAL:	**34 railway cars**	
Rags	400 railway cars	2,700,000 kg.
Bed feathers	130 railway cars	270,000 kg.
Women's hair	1 railway car	3,000 kg.
Reusable material	5 railway cars	19,000 kg.
SUBTOTAL:	**536 railway cars**	**2,992,000 kg.**
TOTAL:	**570 railway cars**	

2. Volksdeutsche Mittelstelle (Ethnic German Aid Office)

Men's Clothing:

Coats	99,000 pieces
Jackets	57,000 pieces
Vests	27,000 pieces
Pants	62,000 pieces
Underwear	38,000 pieces
Shirts	132,000 pieces
Sweaters	9,000 pieces
Scarves	2,000 pieces
Pajamas	6,000 pieces
Collars	10,000 pieces
Socks	10,000 pieces
Shoes	31,000 pieces

Children's Clothing:

Coats	15,000 pieces
Boy's jackets	11,000 pieces
Boy's pants	3,000 pieces
Shirts	3,000 pieces
Scarves	4,000 pieces
Sweaters	1,000 pieces
Underwear	1,000 pieces
Girl's dresses	9,000 pieces
Girl's blouses	5,000 pieces
Aprons	2,000 pieces
Stockings	10,000 pieces
Shoes	22,000 pieces

Women's Clothing:

Coats	155,000 pieces
Dresses	119,000 pieces
Jackets	26,000 pieces
Skirts	30,000 pieces
Shirts	125,000 pieces
Blouses	30,000 pieces
Sweaters	60,000 pieces
Underwear	49,000 pieces
Pajamas	27,000 pieces
Aprons	36,000 pieces
Shoes	111,000 pair

Linen, etc.:

Bed coverings	37,000 pieces
Sheets	46,000 pieces
Pillow cases	75,000 pieces
Tea towels	27,000 pieces
Handkerchiefs	135,000 pieces
Towels	100,000 pieces
Table cloths	11,000 pieces
Napkins	8,000 pieces
Ties	25,000 pieces
Galoshes and boots	24,000 pair
Hats	9,000 pieces

Source: National Archives

A Cartload of Shoes

Abraham Sutzkever was a famous Yiddish poet and editor. Born in 1913 in Belorussia, Sutzkever's family settled in Vilna, then part of Poland, in 1922. He first published poetry in 1934. During the Nazi occupation of Vilna, Sutzkever was prominent among the organizers of the Vilna ghetto underground, encouraging literary activities and ghetto theater. He escaped from the ghetto and joined other partisans fighting in the surrounding forests. Throughout this time, he continued to write poetry and to preserve it. His work from this period was published in Tel Aviv in 1979 under the title *The First Night in the Ghetto*. Also, *Burnt Pearls: Ghetto Poems* was published in 1981 in the United States.

Talk It Over

1. How do shoes contribute to a person's identity? What do your shoes tell the world about you?

2. What does *Berlin* stand for in the poem?

3. Do you think the recipients of the shoes and other clothing and household items from Auschwitz and Majdanek asked, as the poet does, "Oh, tell me, shoes the truth, where were the feet sent?" Why do you think this is so?

A Cartload of Shoes

The wheels are turning, turning,
What are they bringing there?
They are bringing me a cartload
Of quivering footwear.

A cartload like a wedding
In the evening glow;
The shoes—in heaps, dancing
Like people at a ball.

Is it a holiday, a wedding dance?
Or have I been misled?
I know these shoes at a glance
And look at them with dread.

The heels are tapping:
Where to, where to, what in?
From the old Vilna streets
They ship us to Berlin.

I need not ask whose,
But my heart is rent:
Oh, tell me, shoes, the truth,
Where were the feet sent?

The feet of those boots
With buttons like dew,—
The child of those slippers,
The woman of that shoe?

And children's shoes everywhere,
Why don't I see a child?
Why are the bridal shoes there
Not worn by the bride?

Among the children's worn out boots
My mother's shoes so fair!
Sabbath was the only day
She donned this footwear.

And the heels are tapping:
Where to, where to, what in?
From the old Vilna streets
They chase us to Berlin.

—*Abraham Sutzkever*

Teaching the Diary of Anne Frank   Scholastic Professional Books

"A Cartload of Shoes" by Abraham Sutzkever from *Bearing the Unbearable: Yiddish and Polish Poetry in the Ghettoes and Concentration Camps* edited by Frieda W. Aaron. Published by SUNY Press, Albany, 1990. Extensive research failed to locate the author and the copyright holder of this work.

The End of a Life

Teaching About the Unthinkable

Anne made her last diary entry on Tuesday, August 1, 1944, three days before her arrest. She left no further record. What we know about her from August 4, 1944, to her death from typhus in late February or early March 1945 comes to us through the sympathetic words of other prisoners and through the obsessive record keeping of her murderers.

Telling students about Anne Frank's final months is a daunting task for any teacher. Yet it is important for students to understand what happened to Anne and those who hid with her in the Secret Annexe.

After August 1944, the Anne we know in the diary was progressively stripped of everything that made her Anne. In the end she died alone, without clothes, or food, or hope, in the house of horrors the Nazis had built. The effects of loss, starvation, and terror changed her. A brief encounter with her friend Lies, who survived Bergen-Belsen, gives us one last, unbearably harrowing glimpse of Anne. "It wasn't the same Anne," Lies wrote later. "It was a broken girl."

These women, starving and ill, were liberated from Bergen-Belsen by the British Army.

The essential lesson to take away from this saddest of stories is that Anne and millions of others were killed as part of a policy conceived, debated, carried out, and documented by ordinary people. Ordinary people informed on Anne, arrested, deported, imprisoned, and terrorized her. Ordinary people unleashed the deadly diseases that killed her and tens of thousands of other prisoners in Bergen-Belsen by withholding food, water, shelter, and sanitation.

Only by understanding that the Holocaust was carried out by people, not demons, can students begin to understand that people can prevent the horrors of the Holocaust from sweeping the world again.

Discussion Questions

1. Explain, without justifying, why the Franks were deported.

2. Does knowing what happened to Anne after August 1944 affect your feelings about her diary?

3. Did Anne endanger others by what she wrote in her diary? Was the diary an act of resistance? How might the police have used information in the diary to persecute other people?

❖ Response Journal Ideas

- Reread *Terrible Things* and comment on how the story seems to you now.

- Nazi guards at killing centers taunted their prisoners saying, "Even if you survive, no one will believe you when you try to tell them about this place." What would you say to those guards from your perspective more than 50 years later?

- Individuals can make a difference in the world. Who in your community is concerned about racial harmony? Who stands out as a spokesperson for mutual respect? For tolerance? How can others help?

- Write about how you think you would feel visiting the Anne Frank House in Amsterdam, where "visitors can climb the steps behind the bookcase, walk through the rooms where Anne and her family lived, see the photographs of movie stars that Anne put on the walls, and climb up to the attic where Anne and Peter spent time together."

❖ Projects

- Anne edited her diary after she heard a member of the Dutch government-in-exile say in a BBC broadcast that the diaries of ordinary people would be valuable records after the war. Choose one of your Response Journal entries and edit it—arrange the content, check spelling, change wording, and give both the edited and unedited versions to other readers.

- Write a letter to Anne Frank from "Kitty," Anne's name for her diary. The letter should tell her what happened to Kitty after Anne's last entry on August 1, 1944. The letter should include a description of the diary by Miep and Elli and continue to the present day.

- You may prefer to write a personal letter to Anne Frank. In it you may want to tell her how you were changed by reading her diary. Did it make you realize the meaning of prejudice, for example? Did it teach you about a part of history you never before understood? What did the world lose when it lost Anne? What do you feel you have personally lost as a result of Anne's death? What have you gained as a result of what she left behind?

❖ Resource Pages

Discovery and Arrest

In 1963, Otto Frank described the events of the morning of August 4, 1944, when he and the others in the Secret Annexe were arrested. (They were betrayed by an informant, possibly a Dutch cleaning woman.) The following statement was made by Otto Frank in the case against Karl Silberbauer, the arresting officer, an Austrian.

In the morning—it was about 10:30—I was in the Van Pels [Van Daan in the diary] boy's room . . . giving him an English lesson. At the said time a civilian [someone not in uniform] I did not know came into the said room. He was holding a pistol and he aimed it at us. He made us put our hands in the air and searched us for weapons. This man appeared to be a Dutch official of the German . . . [Security Service] in Amsterdam. Then he ordered us to go downstairs. He followed us with his pistol drawn. First we entered the room of the Van Pels family where I saw Mr. and Mrs. Van Pels and also Mr. Pfeffer [Dussel], all of them standing with their hands up. There was a man in civilian clothes there, too, not known to me, also with a drawn pistol.

Then we were all made to go down one floor to where I lived with my family. There I saw my wife and two daughters standing with their hands up. I believe Mr. Kugler [Koophuis] was also in our room, but I am not sure. It may well have been Mr. Kleiman [Kraler]. At the same time, I saw a man in a green uniform, not known to me, who had also drawn his pistol. This man's name, I learned later, was Silberbauer. He ordered me in a curt, barrack-room tone of voice to show him where we kept our money and jewelry. I pointed out where they were. Then he picked up a briefcase in which my daughter Anne kept her papers, including her diary notes. He shook the briefcase out onto the floor and then put our jewelry and our money into it.

The people in the Secret Annexe were allowed a few minutes to pack their clothes. After the police left with their 10 prisoners (Victor Kugler and Johannes Kleiman had been arrested too), Miep and Elli went upstairs to the hiding place, defying the police who had told them to remain in the office. Upstairs they found signs of a hasty departure—drawers wide open, belongings thrown on the floor. Among the things on the floor Miep found Anne's original diary in its orange-red plaid binding, and other notebooks and diary entries on loose sheets of paper. Despite their fear of being caught if the police returned, Elli and Miep picked up as many papers of Anne's as they could find. Downstairs in the office Miep put the papers in a drawer of her desk. She was sure Anne would be back, and she wanted to keep the diary safe for her.

From *The Diary of a Young Girl: The Definitive Edition* by Anne Frank. Otto H. Frank and Mirjam Pressler, editors, translated by Susan Massotty. Translation copyright © 1995 by Doubleday, a division of Bantam Doubleday Dell Publishing Group, Inc. Used by permission of Doubleday, a division of Bantam Doubleday Dell Publishing Group, Inc.

The Last Months

Westerbork

After their arrest, the Franks and Van Pels and Mr. Pfeffer (Alfred Dussel in the diary) were taken first to a prison in Amsterdam and then by passenger train to Westerbork, a transit camp. Kugler and Kleiman were sent to another prison camp in the Netherlands. After the war, Otto Frank recalled that Anne spent the train ride to Westerbork pressed to the window looking out at the meadows, fields, and villages. In Westerbork, the prisoners from the Secret Annexe were more restricted than other prisoners as punishment for having been in hiding. Despite that, an eyewitness reported later that during the month the Franks and Van Pels were in Westerbork, Anne and Peter were seen together often, and Anne seemed very happy.

From 1942 to 1944, 115,000 Dutch Jews were sent either to Westerbork or to another transit camp, Vught, to await transport to Auschwitz and Sobibor. The prisoners from the Secret Annexe were hopeful they would be spared that fate. But on September 3, 1944, they were all packed into cattle cars bound for Auschwitz. They were on the very last transport to leave Westerbork.

Auschwitz

The last transport of Jews from the Netherlands arrived at Auschwitz on September 5. Thanks to the obsessive record keeping of the camp authorities, we know that the transport included 1,019 prisoners: 498 men, 442 women, and 79 children (under 15 years old). Since Anne had celebrated her fifteenth birthday in June, she was counted among the women. Five hundred and forty-nine people, including all the children, were gassed the next day. Among these were Mr. Van Pels, Peter's father. The others were split up—Otto, Peter, and Mr. Pfeffer went to a men's barracks; Anne, Margot, their mother, and Mrs. Van Pels were sent to the women's part of the camp. Otto Frank never saw his wife or daughters again. Conditions at Auschwitz were deliberately designed to break down and dehumanize the prisoners. Prisoners had their heads shaved. Beatings were commonplace; often people were beaten to death in front of other prisoners. Food was scarce, and medical care was nonexistent. Over everyone, all the time, hung the threat of being gassed.

Bergen-Belsen

After less than two months in Auschwitz, Margot and Anne were sent to Bergen-Belsen, a concentration camp in Germany. Bergen-Belsen had never been a killing center. For that reason, earlier in the war, it had seemed to many prisoners a desirable destination. When Anne and Margot arrived, they met several women they had known in Amsterdam. At the end of November, Mrs. Van Pels arrived. Mrs. Frank remained in Auschwitz where she died of disease in early January, a few weeks before the camp was liberated by the Russians.

Bergen-Belsen was not a killing center with gas chambers and crematoria, but by the winter of 1944–1945, it had become a place of death. Thousands of women were sent to Bergen-Belsen from camps in Poland. There wasn't enough housing for so many people. In the horribly overcrowded, unsanitary conditions, tens of thousands of people died from cold, hunger, and infectious diseases. Survivors report that the guards were concerned only with keeping people from escaping; there was no system for distributing food, water, or medicine. In the section of the camp where Anne and Margot were confined during that bitterly cold winter, conditions became increasingly chaotic.

Teaching the Diary of Anne Frank   Scholastic Professional Books

Final Meeting

Among the Dutch prisoners in Bergen-Belsen was Anne's old friend Lies, whom she described in her diary. Lies had been sent with her family to Bergen-Belsen as part of a group intended for a possible prisoner exchange with the Allies. This meant that she was in a different, and far better-off, part of the camp. In late February, Lies found out that Anne was in Bergen-Belsen and arranged to make contact with her.

Lies survived the war and, years later, described her encounter with Anne.

For Lies, the memories of the war are sad and bitter.

Anne came to the barbed-wire fence—I couldn't see her. The fence and the straw [pushed through the barbed wire to make a wall] were between us. There wasn't much light. Maybe I saw her shadow. It wasn't the same Anne. She was a broken girl. I probably was too, but it was so terrible. She immediately began to cry, and she told me, "I don't have any parents anymore."

I remember that with absolute certainty. That was terribly sad, because she couldn't have known anything else. She thought her father had been gassed right away. . . .

So we stood there, two young girls, and we cried. . . . She told me that Margot was seriously ill, and she told me about going into hiding because I was, of course, extremely curious. . . . [Back in Amsterdam, in July 1942, the rumor had spread that the Frank family had fled to safety in Switzerland. The Franks themselves had left clues suggesting this so that no one would hunt for them in hiding.]

Then she said, "We don't have anything at all to eat here, almost nothing, and we are cold; we don't have any clothes and I've gotten very thin and they shaved my hair." That was terrible for her. She had always been very

proud of her hair. It may have grown back a bit in the meantime, but it certainly wasn't the long hair she'd had before, which she playfully curled around her fingers. It was much worse for them than for us. I said, "They didn't take away our clothes." That was our first meeting. [On two subsequent meetings, Lies was able to throw Anne a package with some food in it. The first time someone else caught the package, but on a second attempt, Anne caught the gift from her old friend.]

After these three or four meetings at the barbed wire fence in Bergen-Belsen, I didn't see her again, because the people in Anne's camp were transferred to another section of Bergen-Belsen. That happened around the end of February.

Shortly after Anne's final meeting with Lies, Margot died of typhus. Anne died a few days later, not knowing that her father was alive. He had been liberated from Auschwitz by the Russians in January and was desperate to find his daughters. A few weeks after Anne's death, Bergen-Belsen was liberated by British soldiers.

Excerpt from *The Last Seven Months of Anne Frank* by Willy Lindwer, translated by Alison Meersschaert. Copyright © 1991 by Willy Lindwer. Reprinted by permission of Pantheon Books, a division of Random House, Inc.

After the Diary Ended

Anne Frank Died in Bergen-Belsen, March 1945, of typhus.

Otto Frank Liberated from Auschwitz, January 26, 1945, by Soviet troops. Reached Amsterdam in June 1945 and returned briefly to his old business at 263 Prinsengracht. Increasingly involved in the publication of Anne's diary and in the Anne Frank Foundation, which he established in 1957. Married an Auschwitz survivor and moved to Switzerland in 1953. Died in Switzerland in 1980.

Edith Frank Died in Auschwitz, January 6, 1945.

Margot Frank Died in Bergen-Belsen, March 1945, of typhus.

The real names of others in the Annexe were changed by Otto Frank when he edited the diary.

Mr. Van Pels (Van Daan) Gassed at Auschwitz-Birkenau, September 1945.

Mrs. Van Pels (Van Daan) Sent from Bergen-Belsen to two other camps before she died in April or May 1945.

Peter Van Pels (Van Daan) Forced to march from Auschwitz with tens of thousands of other prisoners in January 1945, away from the advancing Russian army. Thousands died along the way under appalling conditions— shot by the SS or killed by cold and hunger and disease. Peter survived the march, which ended up at Mauthausen concentration camp in Austria. He died there on May 5, three days before the camp was liberated.

Fritz Pfeffer (Alfred Dussel) Died in Neuengamme concentration camp in December 1944.

Miep Gies Still lives in Amsterdam. Her husband Jan (Henk in the diary) died in 1993. Her book *Anne Frank Remembered* was published in 1987. She is featured in the award-winning film of the same name.

Elli (Bep) Vossen Married in 1946; raised a large family and died in 1983.

Mr. Kugler (Kraler) Escaped from prison in Holland in the winter of 1944–1945 and returned home, where he hid until the end of the war. In 1955 he immigrated to Canada, where he died in 1981.

Mr. Kleiman (Koophuis) Returned to Amsterdam after the war and worked in the business, which had moved from the building at 263 Prinsengracht, until his death in 1959.

Anne's Legacy

Otto Frank was liberated from Auschwitz on January 26, 1945, by troops of the advancing Russian army. Before he left Poland, he found out that his wife, Edith, had died in Auschwitz of disease early in January, the same month he was liberated. He also learned that Anne and Margot had been sent to Bergen-Belsen in October 1944. Eventually he made his way back to the Netherlands, traveling by ship, train, and truck, arriving on Miep's doorstep on June 3, 1945. He moved in with Miep and her husband Jan at their insistence and went back to work at his office at 263 Prinsengracht. He tried desperately to get information about Margot and Anne from Dutch survivors of Bergen-Belsen who were returning home. One day Otto Frank learned that Anne and Margot had died in Bergen-Belsen. That same day, Miep gave him Anne's diary. Here's how she describes the moment.

I reached into the drawer on the side of my desk and took out the papers that had been waiting there for Anne for nearly a year now. No one, including me, had touched them. Now Anne was not coming back for her diary.

I took out all the papers, placing the little red-orange checkered diary on top and carried everything into Mr. Frank's office.

[Mr.] Frank was sitting at his desk, his eyes murky with shock. I held out the diary and the papers to him. I said, "Here is your daughter Anne's legacy to you."

Miep Gies resisted reading the diary she had so carefully saved for Anne. Finally, after the second edition of the diary was printed, she waited until she could be alone and then opened the book at last.

I read the whole diary without stopping. From the first word, I heard Anne's voice come back to speak to me from where she had gone. I lost track of time. Anne's voice tumbled out of the book, so full of life, moods, curiosity, feelings. She was no longer gone and destroyed. She was alive again in my mind. . . .

I was thankful I hadn't read the diary after the arrest, during the final nine months of the [Nazi] occupation [of the Netherlands], while it had stayed in my desk drawer right beside me every day. Had I read it, I would have had to burn the diary because it would have been too dangerous for people about whom Anne had written.

When I had read the last word, I didn't feel the pain I had anticipated. I was glad I'd read it at last. The emptiness in my heart was eased. So much had been lost, but now Anne's voice would never be lost. My young friend had left a remarkable legacy to the world.

But always, every day of my life, I've wished that things had been different. That even had Anne's diary been lost to the world, Anne and the others might somehow have been saved.

Not a day goes by that I do not grieve for them.

Talk It Over

1. Why do you think Miep Gies was reluctant to read Anne's diary even after it had been published?

2. In what way was the diary "dangerous" for Miep to keep during the Nazi occupation?

3. How do you explain the diary's worldwide popularity? What is universal in Anne's story?

Teaching the Diary of Anne Frankt Through Her Diary   Scholastic Professional Books

The Diary in the World

After Otto Frank read Anne's diary in the summer of 1945, he told others about it and translated parts of it into German for his relatives in Switzerland. Friends urged him to have the diary published, but at first no publishers were interested. Then in 1946, "A Child's Voice," an article about Anne's diary, appeared in a Dutch newspaper. The article interested a Dutch publisher. The first edition of Anne's diary appeared in the summer of 1947. It was then called *Het Achterhuis*, which means "the house behind," or, in English, the "secret annexe."

The diary was first translated into French and German; an English edition, *The Diary of a Young Girl*, was published in 1951. Since then Anne's diary has been translated into 55 languages, and more than 20 million copies of the book have been sold. The play and movie, *The Diary of Anne Frank*, and a television drama, *The Attic*, have also brought Anne's story to millions of people around the world.

The Diary Today

When Otto Frank died in 1980, he left Anne's original diaries and other manuscripts to the Netherlands State Institute for War Documentation. To answer questions that had been raised about the diary, the institute asked the State Forensic Science Laboratory to analyze the handwriting and materials (ink, binding, paper) used in the manuscripts. The report was published in the Netherlands in 1986 and in the United States in 1988 as part of *The Diary of Anne Frank: The Critical Edition* (1988). The report states: "as far as we are concerned there is not the slightest reason to doubt either the authenticity of the manuscripts or the intrinsic quality of *The Diary of Anne Frank*."

The Diary of Anne Frank: The Critical Edition contains three versions of the diary. The first is Anne's original diary. The second is the edited diary she prepared after hearing the Dutch cabinet minister say that diaries would be valuable after the war (March 29, 1944). The third is the published diary, which was edited by Otto Frank when he typed the manuscript for publication.

Teaching the Diary of Anne Frank   Scholastic Professional Books

The Anne Frank House and the Anne Frank Foundation

Every year about 600,000 people from around the world visit the building at 263 Prinsengracht in Amsterdam where Anne and her family hid for over two years. The Anne Frank House was opened to the public in 1960 by the Anne Frank Foundation, created by Otto Frank.

Visitors can climb the steps behind the bookcase, walk through the rooms where Anne and her family lived, see the photographs of movie stars that Anne put on the walls, and climb up to the attic where Anne and Peter spent time together.

Exhibits in other parts of the building display the original diaries and deal with current issues of anti-Semitism and intolerance. The Anne Frank Foundation also sponsors educational projects for teachers, students, and social workers. These activities are undertaken in the spirit of applying Anne's message of tolerance to issues of the present day.

Anne Frank Center USA

The Anne Frank Center USA brings the legacy of Anne Frank to life across the United States through exhibitions and educational programs. The center's activities focus on its traveling exhibits, which relate the story of the Franks through family photographs, Anne's diary, and documents of the Holocaust. The core of the center's mission is to use Anne Frank's story as a catalyst for community organization, collaboration, and discussion about current issues of tolerance and prejudice. By providing local organizations with ways to use the exhibit as the centerpiece of a month-long community event, the center empowers citizens from all walks of life to initiate meaningful community dialogue on the sensitive issues of discrimination and violence and to find ways to combat hate.

Extension Projects and Resources

These activities can expand students' understanding of the major themes in the diary and help them explore in more depth some of the key events and issues of the Holocaust.

Listen to the Survivors

Holocaust survivors in many communities are willing to visit schools to share their memories and insights with young people. Arrange to have a visitor come and invite students' parents to visit at the same time. Prepare for the visit by gathering materials, such as a map of Europe, sample entries from students' Response Journals, and a list of questions. A team of students can create a formal written invitation, explaining what they have been studying. Be sure to tell your guest how long he or she will have to speak and take questions. After the visit, students can write individual thank-you letters.

Locate survivors through local Jewish congregations, senior citizen centers, Jewish organizations, or Holocaust centers in many large cities. Survivors of the Shoah Visual History Foundation is Steven Spielberg's ongoing oral history project. Volunteers and workers in several countries are filming interviews with Holocaust survivors, who speak about their experiences. Because of this project, firsthand testimony about the Holocaust will be forever available even when the survivors, many of whom are elderly, are no longer alive. Some critics of the project say the subject is too overwhelming for any such attempt to be effective. Ask a team of students to research the Shoah oral history project or similar projects that local organizations are involved in.

Share Your Response Journals

Make your last entries in the Response Journal, evaluating the experience of keeping the journal. Review earlier entries and write comments on the pages reserved for that purpose. Choose some of your best entries and combine them with students' selections to create a public journal. Use a bulletin board or display case in your school to show others how you and your students used the journals to help you understand Anne's diary and the materials on the Holocaust.

Go Back to the Home Front—1942–1944

What was it like to be a teenager in the United States in the years 1942–1944, the same period that Anne was in hiding? To find out, assign students to interview people who were teenagers in 1942 to 1944. The researchers can also use contemporary reference materials such as *Life* magazine for visual impressions of the period. In their reports, students can contrast the interests of American teenagers of the time with those of Anne Frank.

Make Connections

Using history books, newspapers, and on-line resources, have students investigate past and present instances of officially sanctioned intolerance and genocide. (For example, slavery in the United States, apartheid in South Africa, tribal conflicts in Rwanda, ethnic cleansing in Bosnia, and the killing fields of Cambodia.) What was the effect on the victims, the perpetrators, and those seemingly uninvolved—both individuals and nations? Throughout history, governments and individuals have imposed harsh policies just as there were times when individuals and governments could actively condemn such policies—or do nothing.

"I was just following orders."

Many defendants during the war crimes trials at Nuremberg claimed they were "just following orders" in carrying out the policies of the Holocaust. Even recently, former Nazis living in the United States. and other countries have used that excuse for having murdered civilians during World War II. Can students explain the moral emptiness of following orders to kill innocent people? Is there a difference between what the Nazis did and what soldiers are trained to do in wartime? (For more information, see The Nuremberg Trials on page 99.)

Surviving Nazi leaders went on trial in Nuremberg.

Combat Hate

The Anne Frank Center USA states that its traveling exhibit, *Anne Frank in the World 1929–1945*, "empowers citizens from all walks of life to initiate meaningful community dialogue on the sensitive issues of discrimination and violence and to find ways to combat hate."

Your class can spur action by brainstorming with other students, teachers, and community members about the issues that separate people in your community. What would be the rules of conduct for a meaningful community dialogue? Whom would you invite to exchange?

What role can young people play in bringing harmony to the community? Find out more about the *Anne Frank in the World* exhibit by visiting the Anne Frank Center USA's Web site (www.annefrank.com) or by writing for information: Anne Frank Center USA, 584 Broadway, Suite 408, New York, NY 10012.

Elie Wiesel

"What would future generations say about us . . . if we do nothing?"

On December 13, 1995, Elie Wiesel, Auschwitz survivor, author, and tireless advocate for human rights, appeared with President Bill Clinton at the White House. Wiesel (wee-ZELL) supported the president's decision to send U.S. troops to Bosnia. They were sent to enforce a peace agreement reached in Dayton, Ohio. In introducing Elie Wiesel, President Clinton quoted the citation that accompanied Wiesel's Nobel Peace Prize in 1984: "Elie Wiesel . . . is a messenger to mankind. He is a passionate witness to humanity's capacity for the worst, and a powerful example of humanity's capacity for the best."

In his remarks about Bosnia, Elie Wiesel said:

We in the United States represent a certain moral aspect of history. A great nation owes its greatness not only to its military power, but also to its moral consciousness, awareness. What would future generations say about us, all of us here in this land, if we do nothing [about the bloodshed in the former Yugoslavia]? After all, people were dying, people were killing each other, day after day.

As students consider the situation in the former Yugoslavia referred to by Elie Wiesel, have them read *Zlata's Diary: A Child's Life in Sarajevo* by Zlata Filipovic, a dramatic chronicle of a young girl and her family during the bombardment of Sarjevo by Serbia. Have students note similarities between Zlata's diary and Anne Frank's.

Could It Happen Again?

"Eternal vigilance is the price of liberty." What do students think this means? What does *vigilance* mean? What does *liberty* mean? What does the statement mean for us today? Can we ever let down our guard where prejudice is concerned? Are there any recent events that prove or disprove this statement? Give examples of present-day vigilance against intolerance and discrimination in the United States. What protections do U.S. citizens have? Could we give up those protections as the Germans did? (They had a democratic government until Hitler came to power.)

They Fought Back

Jewish partisans, like Jenny Misuchin, escaped the ghettos of Eastern Europe and fought the Nazis from forests, swamps, and mountains. People inside the ghettos also fought back against the Germans in Warsaw, Vilna, Krakow, Kovno, and other cities. Armed revolt took place even in killing centers at Treblinka, Sobibor, and Auschwitz.

Have students work together in small groups to prepare reports on what they can find out about these resistance movements. Each report should answer these questions: Who took part? What were the connections between the Jewish fighters and the non-Jewish partisans and residents of the country? What effect did these actions have on the Nazis who were carrying out the Holocaust? Students can also consider the tradition of resistance in stories from Jewish history, such as the story of Masada and Chanukah. Think about this quotation from the Passover seder: "In every generation a tyrant has risen to destroy us."

Rescue in Denmark

With the help of the Danish resistance and thousands of ordinary Danes, 6,000 Jews, 1,300 part-Jews, and 680 non-Jewish family members were transported by boat from Denmark to neutral Sweden at the end of September and the beginning of October 1943. This united action, carried out under the noses of the Nazis, saved the overwhelming majority of Danish Jews. Assign students to discover more about the rescue of Danish Jews. Ask them to dramatize a brief scene in which a Danish bystander decides to become a participant.

Students can find some answers in the novel *Number the Stars* by Lois Lowry and the non-fiction book *A Place to Hide: True Stories of Holocaust Rescues* by Jayne Pettit.

Anne Frank's *Tales of the Secret Annex*

Anne's short stories and essays, written during the same period as her diary, have been published in Anne Frank's *Tales From the Secret Annex* (Bantam Books, 1994). Ask for volunteers to dramatize (write a short play and then present it) one of the writings from this book.

The Nuremberg Trials

Five months after World War II ended in Europe, an international military tribunal created by the victorious Allies began the trials of leading Nazis. The tribunal was made up of two judges from each of the Allied nations—the United States, Great Britain, France, and the Soviet Union. On October 6, 1945, the judges officially charged 24 German civilian and military leaders with four categories of crimes. Their trials were held at Nuremberg, Germany, the site of massive Nazi Party rallies and the place where the Nuremberg Laws restricting Jewish civil rights were announced.

The categories of crimes tried by the tribunal were conspiracy, crimes against international peace, war crimes, and crimes against humanity. The fourth category included crimes committed against Jews and others in Germany and Nazi-occupied Europe: "murder, extermination, enslavement, deportation, and other inhumane acts committed against any civilian population [during the war] . . . persecutions on political, racial, or religious grounds . . . whether or not in violation of domestic law of the country where perpetrated." Categories three and four were the areas in which prosecutors were most successful in gaining convictions.

The verdicts were announced on October 1, 1946. The judges convicted 19 of the defendants. Twelve of those convicted were sentenced to death. Ten were executed two weeks later. But two men sentenced to death cheated the hangman. One, Hermann Goering, the founder of the Gestapo, commander of the air force, and one of Hitler's trusted advisers, committed suicide before his execution. The other, Martin Bormann, Hitler's private secretary and confidant, was not at the trial. He had disappeared in April 1945 and was tried and convicted in absentia.

Between November 1946 and April 1949, more trials, involving 185 defendants, were held at Nuremberg under the authority of the United States, one of the four powers occupying Germany.

Glossary

Allies Britain, France, the Soviet Union, and the United States, which fought against Germany, Italy, and Japan, referred to as the Axis.

Anschluss [ON-shluss] Annexation; refers to the March 12, 1938, annexation of Austria by Germany.

Anti-Semitism Systematic prejudice against Jews.

Aryan Under the Nazis, this word was applied to a mythical Germanic race and given an underpinning of validity by pseudoscientific definitions.

Auschwitz [OWSH-vitch] The German name for Oswiecim, a city in Poland that was the site of one of the largest of the Nazi killing centers (Auschwitz-Birkenau) as well as a concentration camp and labor camp for I. G. Farben.

Babi Yar [bobby-YAR] A deep ravine outside the Ukrainian city of Kiev where 34,000 Jews were killed in September 1941 by mobile killing units (*einsatzgruppen*) advancing with the German army.

Chelmno Generally thought to be the first of the six death camps in Poland.

Concentration camp Barracks and other structures built at the beginning of the Third Reich to house "enemies of the Third Reich." Concentration camps had various purposes: Some were labor camps, some were prison camps, others were transit camps, and the most infamous were death camps or killing centers.

Death camps (killing centers) A concentration camp built for the purpose of killing the inmates. The death camps associated with the Holocaust were in Poland: Auschwitz-Birkenau, Belzek, Chelmno, Madjanek, Sobibor, Treblinka.

Deportation During the Holocaust, this term was a euphemism for the removal of Jews either from their homes to a ghetto or from a ghetto to a killing center.

Einsatzgruppen [INE-sats-groopen] Mobile killing units ("task groups") that operated during the invasion of the Soviet Union. Their purpose was to kill Jews and others deemed undesirable by the Third Reich.

Final solution Nazi euphemism for the plan to kill the Jews of Europe. Part of the elaborate coded language devised and used by the Nazi command to keep the German people and the intended victims ignorant of the plan.

Genocide [JEN-o-side] The deliberate annihilation of an entire people or nation.

Gestapo [guess-TOP-oh] The internal security police of the Third Reich; charged with protecting the regime from political opposition. Under Heinrich Himmler's command, the Gestapo enjoyed broad investigative powers into every aspect of German life.

Ghetto A walled section of a city in which Jews were forced to live in medieval times.

Holocaust From a Hebrew word meaning "burnt offering."

Judenrat [YOU-den-raht] Nazi-appointed Jewish community authority, ultimately required to choose Jews for transports to the killing centers..

Kristallnacht [KRIS-tal-nakht] Meaning "night of broken glass," it refers to organized attacks by Nazis and their followers against Jewish property, synagogues, and individuals on November 9, 1938. In the aftermath, "for their own protection," Jews were arrested and sent to concentration camps.

Nazi, National Socialist German Workers' Party [NOT-zee] A political party taken over by Adolf Hitler in the 1920s. In 1933, after an indecisive election, Hitler took over the government and established the Third Reich. The Nazi Party became the sole political party in Germany.

Nuremberg A city in Germany where the Reichstag (legislature) met in September 1935 to pass the Nuremberg Laws, which gave legal status to the Nazis' racial mythology. Ten years later, the International Military Tribunal held war crimes trials there.

Pogrom [poe-GROM] An organized, systematic discriminatory action against Jews.

SS "Protection squads." Originally referred to Hitler's elite guard. Eventually the SS were put in charge of the death camps.

Shoah [SHOW-ah] "Desolation" in Hebrew; a word used to refer to the Holocaust.

Swastika [SWAH-stick-ah] An ancient symbol adapted by the National Socialist (Nazi) Party in Germany and identified as a symbol of Nazism ever since.

Third Reich [Rike] The name for the Nazi regime in Germany from the end of 1933 to 1945.

Wannsee Conference [VAHN-zay] A conference held on January 20, 1942, in Berlin, at which an action plan for the total annihilation of European Jews was established.

Yad Vashem [Yahd-Vah-SHEM] A museum in Israel dedicated to Holocaust victims.

Resources

Books

ANNE FRANK Grade 5 and up

The Diary of a Young Girl by Anne Frank (Bantam, 1993) For more than 50 years, this book has engaged readers with its poignant revelations of an engaging young girl's coming of age under extraordinarily difficult conditions.

Anne Frank's Tales from the Secret Annex by Anne Frank (Bantam, 1994)

Anne Frank: Beyond the Diary, A Photographic Remembrance by Rud van der Rol and Rian Verhoeven (Scholastic, 1995) Stunning photographs compiled by the Anne Frank House in Amsterdam bring us images of Anne Frank's life from birth to 1942, when she and her family went into hiding. Images of the concentration camps and quotations from those imprisoned with Anne complete her story.

ANNE FRANK Grade 7 and up

Anne Frank Remembered: The Story of the Woman Who Helped to Hide the Frank Family by Miep Gies (Simon & Schuster, 1988) Miep Gies played a crucial role in the hiding of the Frank family and four others in Amsterdam from 1942 to 1944. Her story amplifies and sheds light on Anne Frank's diary.

The Last Seven Months of Anne Frank by Willy Lindwer (Anchor, 1992) The months between Anne Frank's arrest in August 1944 and her death in 1945 are chronicled here by the Dutch women (then teenagers) who were imprisoned with her in Westerbork, Auschwitz, and Bergen-Belsen.

ANNE FRANK Grade 9 and up

Anne Frank: The Biography by Melissa Mueller (Metropolitan Books, 1998) This first adult biography of Anne Frank contains five pages of Anne's diary that her father had removed. The book, based on extensive research, puts Anne's experiences in a historical context and contains an epilogue by Miep Geis.

HISTORIES Grade 5 and up

Hitler's War Against the Jews—the Holocaust: A Young Reader's Version of the War Against the Jews 1933–1945 by Lucy Dawidowicz (Behrman House, 1978) Lucy Dawidowicz's groundbreaking work, which demonstrated that the destruction of the Jews was Hitler's main goal, has been shortened and simplified.

A Nightmare in History: The Holocaust 1933–1945 by Miriam Chaikin (Houghton Mifflin, 1987) Personal stories and excerpts from diaries put human faces on the step-by-step process that ended in the annihilation of Europe's Jews.

Warsaw Ghetto Uprising by Elaine Landau (Macmillan, 1992) Graphic text and photographs focus on the 28-day battle in the Warsaw ghetto.

Never to Forget: The Jews of the Holocaust by Milton Meltzer (Dell, 1977) Meltzer covers anti-Semitism and Jewish resistance in one of the most valuable Holocaust histories written for young people.

Rescue: The Story of How Gentiles Saved Jews in the Holocaust by Milton Meltzer (HarperCollins, 1991) Excerpts from diaries, letters, interviews, and eyewitness accounts tell these stories of personal courage in the face of evil.

The Holocaust: A History of Courage and Resistance by Bea Stadtier (Behrman House, 1975) The author highlights examples of Jewish resistance to the Holocaust.

HISTORIES Grade 7 and up

"Hitler's Horrors," U.S. News & World Report, Special Report: 50 Years Later, April 3, 1995. This special issue of the news-magazine succinctly depicts the war and chronicles Hitler's years in power.

"The Last Days of Auschwitz," Newsweek, January 16, 1995. The article looks back 50 years to the liberation of Auschwitz and describes untold stories from that time.

HISTORIES Grade 9 and up

The Destruction of the European Jews (student edition). by Raul Hilberg (Holmes and Meier, 1985) This is a shortened ver-sion of Hilberg's classic three-volume study of the destruction process, from racial laws to killing centers.

Historical Atlas of the Holocaust, United States Holocaust Memorial Museum (Macmillan, 1996) More than 230 full-color maps and accompanying text tell the story of the distribution of Jews and Gypsies before the war, through deportations, concen-tration camps, killing centers, death marches, and armed resistance.

The Holocaust: The Fate of European Jewry, 1932–1945 by Leni Yahil (Oxford, 1991) This landmark Holocaust history is beautifully written, exhaustively documented, and equipped with an excellent index.

They Fought Back: The Story of Jewish Resistance in Nazi Europe by Yuri Suhl (Schocken Books, 1975) Accounts of Jewish resistance across Nazi Europe.

The Holocaust: Final Judgment by Victor Bernstein (Macmillan, 1980) The documents used to make the case against war criminals at Nuremberg.

Justice at Nuremberg by Robert E. Conot (Carroll & Graf, 1984) Details the preparations for the trials as well as the trials themselves.

Lest Innocent Blood Be Shed: The Story of the Village of Le Chambon, and How Goodness Happened There by Philip Hallie (Harper, 1979) The story of the Christian townspeople of Le Chambon, France, who risked their lives to hide Jewish families.

BIOGRAPHIES AND MEMOIRS Grades 6 and up

***In Kindling Flame: The Story of Hannah Senesh 1921–1944*
by Linda Atkinson** (William Morrow, 1992) Resistance fighter
Senesh left a secure life on a kibbutz in Palestine to return to
Hungary on a rescue mission during the Holocaust. The book contains excerpts from Hannah Senesh's writings, historical background, and an account of her capture and execution by the Nazis.

***I Am a Star: Child of the Holocaust* by Inge Auerbacher**
(Prentice Hall, 1987) A personal account told in poetry and prose
of the author's three years of childhood in a concentration camp.
Illustrated with drawings and photographs.

***Tell Them We Remember: The Story of the Holocaust* by
Susan D. Bachrach** (Little, Brown, 1994) Based on the U.S.
Holocaust Memorial Museum's permanent exhibition, the book
details how the lives of 20 children were affected by the Holocaust.

***Hitler: Portrait of a Tyrant* by Albert Marrin** (Viking, 1987)
The most detailed account of Hitler and Nazism available in books
for young people.

***Raoul Wallenberg* by Michael Nicholson and David Winner**
(Morehouse, 1990) In the history of Holocaust rescues, the name
of Raoul Wallenberg, a Swedish diplomat, is a shining beacon. This
is the only biography of Wallenberg for young readers.

***A Place to Hide: True Stories of Holocaust Rescues* by
Jayne Pettit** (Scholastic, 1993) The "quiet" rescuers—from Miep
Gies to Oskar Schindler, from the rescuers of Danish Jews to the
village of Le Chambon in southern France—who risked their lives
to save others are honored in this book.

***The Upstairs Room* by Johanna Reiss** (HarperCollins, 1990)
During the Holocaust, Reiss, then a 12-year-old, hid with her older
sister in the farmhouse of a Dutch family. A sequel, *The Journey
Back*, continues the story after the war.

***The Cage* by Ruth M. Sender** (Macmillan, 1986) This graphic
story begins just before the Nazi invasion of Poland and chronicles
the author's life as a child in the Lodz ghetto and at Auschwitz. *To
Life*, a sequel, continues the author's story from liberation to her
arrival in the United States.

BIOGRAPHIES AND MEMOIRS Grades 7 and up

***Night* by Elie Wiesel** (Bantam, 1982) At age 14, Elie Wiesel was
transported to Auschwitz, where his mother and sister were killed.
This compelling memoir has become required reading for those
who want to learn about the Holocaust.

BIOGRAPHIES AND MEMOIRS Grade 9 and up

***Schindler's List* by Thomas Keneally** (Simon & Schuster, 1992)
Based on interviews with Jews saved by Oskar Schindler.

RELATED MEMOIR

***Zlata's Diary: A Child's Life in Sarajevo* by Zlata Filipovic**
(Viking Penguin, 1994) From age 11 to 13, Zlata recorded the
events in her life as a schoolgirl in Sarajevo—from peaceful pas-
times in 1991 to the terror of days in hiding as Serbian guns bom-
barded the city. Zlata's story resonates with implications for
innocent victims of war in every time and place.

FICTION Grade 5 and up

***Terrible Things: An Allegory of the Holocaust* by Eve
Bunting** (Jewish Publication Society, 1993) Though simply told,
this story of how the Terrible Things of the title come for the animals in the clearing has profound implications for defining
"bystander," "victim," and "resister."

***Jacob's Rescue: A Holocaust Story* by Malka Drucker and
Michael Halperin** (Bantam, 1993) Eight-year-old Jacob and his
younger brother David are rescued from the Warsaw ghetto and
hidden by sympathetic Poles.

***Number the Stars* by Lois Lowry** (Houghton Mifflin, 1990) This
1990 Newbery Medal winner tells the story of the rescue of
Danish Jews from the point of view of two young friends, a Jew
and a Gentile. The author incorporates factual details in a thrilling,
well-crafted story of extraordinary bravery.

***Daniel's Story* by Carol Matas** (Scholastic, 1993) More than
one million children suffered in the Holocaust. Their experiences
inspired this novel.

***Friedrich* by Hans P. Richter** (Puffin Books, 1987) The tragic
story of two German boys, one of whom is Jewish, whose friend-
ship is destroyed after the Nazis come to power.

FICTION Grade 7 and up

***I Am Rosemarie* by Marietta Moskin** (Dell, 1987) This novel is
based on the real stories of survivors. Rosemarie was deported
with her family to the Westerbork transit camp and eventually to
Bergen-Belsen.

FICTION Grade 9 and up

***Maus*, Vols. 1 & 2 by Art Spiegelman** (Pantheon, 1993) This
winner of a Pulitzer prize uses cartoon characters to depict the
experiences of the author's parents during the Holocaust and
afterward. Jews are portrayed as mice; the Nazis are represented
as cats.

ART Grade 5 and up

***Children We Remember* by Chana Abells** (Greenwillow, 1986)
Photographs from the collection at Yad Vashem, the Holocaust
memorial in Israel, create a moving record of European Jewish
children.

ART Grade 7 and up

***Rose Blanche* by Roberto Innocenti** (Stewart Tabori & Chang,
1991) An artistic expression of the Holocaust that conveys a
child's failure to understand or accept the events that take place
around her.

***I Never Saw Another Butterfly: Children's Drawings and
Poems from Terezin Concentration Camp 1942–1944*, edited by Hana Volavkova** (Schocken, 1993) Fifteen thousand children passed through Terezin concentration camp between 1942
and 1944. Some of their drawings, paintings, and poems are collected and presented in this book.

ART Grade 9 and up

***The Auschwitz Album: A Book Based Upon an Album Discovered by a Concentration Camp Survivor, Lili Meier* by Peter Hellman** (Random House, 1981) In 1944, an anonymous SS photographer documented the arrival of Hungarian Jews at Auschwitz. The sensitive text by Peter Hellman puts the collection in context.

POETRY Grade 7 and up

***Art from the Ashes*, edited by Lawrence L. Langer** (Oxford University Press, 1995)

***Holocaust Poetry* by Hilda Schiff** (St. Martin's Press, 1995)

On-line Resources

ftp.nizkor.org This is a list of major research centers. Among the Web sites you can access from it are:

Anne Frank Online From the Anne Frank Center USA, information about the diarist

Cybrary of the Holocaust Comprehensive resource includes teaching guide

Nizkor Project Research refuting Holocaust deniers

Simon Wiesenthal Center Excellent resources promoting tolerance

U.S. Holocaust Memorial Museum Information about Washington, DC, museum

CD-ROM Grades 8 and up

Survivors: Testimonies of the Holocaust, 1998. (Knowledge Adventure, 800-545-7677; 19840 Pioneer Ave., Torrance, CA 90503. fax: 310-793-4307. $69.95, includes resource materials) Produced by Steven Spielberg. Four Holocaust survivors tell about their lives before, during, and after World War II.

Videos

Anne Frank Remembered, 2 hr 2 min, 1995 Directed by Jon Blair. Told with family photographs and never-before-seen home movie footage. With moving commentaries from Anne's father, Miep Gies, her friend Hannah Pick-Goslar ("Lies"), and others.

Genocide, 1941–1945 (World At War, vol. 20), 52 min, 1982. (Arts and Entertainment 800-423-1212; A&E Home Video, P.O. Box 2284, South Burlington, VT 05407) Uses archival footage and testimonies.

The Hiding Place, 2 hr 25 min, 1975 Directed by James F. Collier and starring Julie Harris and Eileen Heckart. The story of two Dutch women sent to a concentration camp for hiding Jews during the Holocaust. Based on a true story.

Witness to the Holocaust (Two-video set), 2 hr 10 min, 1984 (Anti-Defamation League, 823 United Nations Plaza, New York, NY 10017) Produced by the Holocaust Education Project for Zachor: National Jewish Resource Center. This video can be shown as seven individual segments, each about 20 minutes long.

Grade 7 and up

The Wannsee Conference, 1 hr 27 min, 1984 Keinz Schirk. The text of this drama is based on the chilling minutes of the conference held at Wannsee in January 1942 where Nazi bureaucrats dispassionately discussed the "final solution." In German with subtitles.

Grade 9 and up

Flames in the Ashes, 1 hr 30 min, 1986 (Ergo Media, Inc. 800-695-3746; P.O. Box 2037, Teaneck, NJ 07666) Resistance to the Nazis by Jews is documented through historic footage and comments by both resisters and their enemies. In Hebrew, Yiddish, French, Italian, and Polish with English subtitles.

Partisans of Vilna, 2 hr 10 min, 1987 (Zenger Video, 800-421-4246; 10200 Jefferson Boulevard, P.O. Box 802, Culver City, CA 90232-0802) Produced by Aviva Kempner. Directed by Josh Waletzky. In 40 moving survivor interviews, the film tells the story of Jewish resistance in the Vilna ghetto. Shows the prominent role women played in the Vilna resistance. An important film best suited for more advanced students of the Holocaust. In Hebrew, Yiddish, and English with subtitles.

Schindler's List, 3 hr 17 min, 1993 (Social Studies School Service, 800-421-4246; 10200 Jefferson Blvd., Room J2, P.O. Box 802, Culver City, CA, 90232-0802) Directed by Steven Spielberg. The film tells the true story of Oskar Schindler. The film contains scenes of graphic violence and nudity. A study guide is available from Facing History and Ourselves (16 Hurd Rd., Brookline, MA 02146-6919).

Organizations

The Anne Frank Center, USA (584 Broadway, Suite 408, New York, NY 10012; 212-431-7993; fax: 212-431-8375) maintains an Exhibition and Education Center and Library. The center is the official North American representative of the Anne Frank House, Amsterdam, and exclusive distributor of Anne Frank House Publications.

The Anti-Defamation League of B'nai B'rith (823 United Nations Plaza, New York, NY 10017) supplies teaching materials such as *The Record—The Holocaust in History, 1933–1945*, published in cooperation with the National Council for Social Studies, 1978.

Facing History and Ourselves (16 Hurd Rd., Brookline, MA 02146-6919) is an organization that provides educators with information and staff development on racism, prejudice, and anti-Semitism

Teaching Tolerance (400 Washington Ave., Montgomery, AL 36104; fax: 334-264-3121) is a magazine published twice a year by the Southern Poverty Law Center and distributed free to educators. The center produces a curriculum kit, *Us and Them*. It is free to schools but must be ordered by principals.

United States Holocaust Memorial Museum Resource Center for Educators (100 Raoul Wallenberg Place, SW, Washington, DC 20004-2150; 202-488-2661; fax 202-488-6137) has a fine collection of curricula, literature, and audiovisual materials for educators. A collection of teaching aids, *Teaching About the Holocaust: Resource Book for Educators*, is available free.